You
Can
Stay
Alive!!

You Can Stay Alive!!

Larry J. Wells
Roger D. Giles

Wilderness Living & Emergency Survival

International Standard Book Number
0-88290-181-8

Library of Congress Card Catalog Number
81-80952

Horizon Publishers' Catalog and Order Number
1228

Fourth Printing, March 1991

Printed and distributed
in the United States of America by

**Horizon
Publishers
& Distributors, Incorporated**
P.O. Box 490 Bountiful, Utah 84011-0490

Preface

If you are an avid backpacker, a cross-country skier, a hunter, a snowmobiler, or just someone who enjoys the outdoors, this book is dedicated to you and your well-being. Though you might not like to think about it, there's always a chance of getting lost backpacking, breaking a ski on a cross-country trek, or having a mechanical breakdown in your snowmobile or vehicle miles from civilization. Things *can* and *do* go wrong. Then you'll know what it means to "be prepared"—or maybe unprepared.

Survival is no accident. That's what this book is really about—staying alive. This book focuses on what to do in emergencies, summer or winter, and how to "be prepared" to stay alive in almost any wilderness crisis situation when the unexpected happens.

This book can save the lives of outdoorsmen—perhaps your life—by telling you what to do in an emergency. It also has tips on wilderness living and safe wilderness travel; how to cross swift streams, large snowfields without proper equipment, where the warmest and safest campsites are found, and many other wilderness tips learned from years of wilderness living experience.

Contents

What To Do First

Controlling Fear and Panic

On a backpacking trip alone, you suddenly see something you've seen before. "That shouldn't be here!" you think. "I passed that old tree five miles back when I dropped off the trail." Taking out your compass, the north arrow points toward what you think is south. "That's not right!" You look around again. Indeed, something isn't right. Slowly, icy fingers start to reach up your neck and into your mind, sending a violent shudder down your spine. Your mouth goes dry, your heart speeds up. A large knot forms in your stomach. You're lost!

Dealing with the first signs of panic is like treating a snakebite. We all know we should remain calm, to minimize the effect of the toxic venom. Most snakebite kits say something like, "You've just been bitten by a snake. Sit down, relax, and read these directions. . . ." Unfortunately, the common reaction is to take off running in a state of blind panic—the worst thing to do. In a panic, people run and even throw away everything that could keep them alive, thinking irrationally they can't move quickly with all their gear. So they throw it away—trying desperately to find their way.

Panic is a venom, but it can be controlled. It's up to you.

Rule Number One: Sit down! The instant you think you have a serious problem—when feelings of uneasiness or anxiety start—*sit down.* You can't run when you're sitting. Stay seated as you think your situation out. Sit down and tie your shoelaces together in knots so you can't run even if you want to. Not only will this give you time to calm yourself, but it will give you something to do and will keep you from running very far.

If you still feel a need to *do* something, build a small fire. This will keep you occupied; and a fire is psychologically very comforting.

Rule Number Two: Channel your thoughts. While you're sitting down, look around. Get control of yourself. This might be a bad situation, but if you can feel the serenity of the land, you can calm yourself. Observe the beauty and peace of nature, then talk to the Creator through prayer. Prayer has been an important strength for most of the people who have been rescued from dangerous situations.

Rule Number Three: Take time to think.

1. Retrace your steps in your mind—where you've been, what you've done.

2. Try to face fear rationally. The greatest fear is fear of the unknown, the fear in our own minds. Are you afraid of discomfort, animals, or being alone? Do you fear the dark, or your own weakness? Are you afraid of something real? Something imaginary?

3. Decide what to do from here. Chart a plan.

In summary, the important thing is to do whatever helps you *stay in control.* No matter how bad a situation, panic will make it worse. It's a dangerous killer, so don't let it engulf you.

Maintaining Body Temperature

The maintenance of proper internal body temperature is the most important factor in determining whether you will survive. Even in extreme heat or cold, internal body temperature (core temperature) seldom varies more than two degrees above or below normal (98.6°F.). If the body's core temperature rises above 109 degrees F., or falls below 84 degrees F., death usually results.

Whenever the body produces heat or absorbs heat from its environment in excessive amounts, and is unable to get rid of it, heat disease results. When the body cannot produce enough heat to maintain its core temperature, it goes into hypothermia. Both are dangerous and very real killers.

Cold

Hypothermia can strike anywhere, and anytime the temperature is below 60 degrees F. It usually strikes in the spring and fall, when people aren't dressed for the cold, particularly when it's raining and temperatures are ranging between 35 and 50 degrees. The people you read or hear about who died from "exposure" or "the elements" probably died of hypothermia. Our bodies have an actual thermostat located in a small piece of nerve tissue at the base of the brain. It controls the production or dissipation of heat, and monitors all parts of the body in order to maintain a constant temperature. When the body starts to go into hypothermia, the body thermostat orders heat to be drawn from the extremities into the core. The body's core temperature must be maintained.

As the body core temperature drops, the body also draws heat from the head. When this happens, circulation slows down, and the victim doesn't get the oxygen or sugar the brain requires. The sugar the brain ordinarily feeds on is being burned to produce heat. As the brain begins to slow down, irrational behavior results. The victim no longer knows what he is doing. This condition comes on so gradually he doesn't realize it's happening. The ability to reason deteriorates. He no longer cares if he lives, and he is unable to take care of himself. Unless the victim receives immediate help, death follows quickly.

To understand how to prevent hypothermia, it is important to understand the mechanics of heat loss.

Heat leaves the body by four basic means:

1. *Evaporation.* Moisture and heat leave the body when we perspire and breathe. The evaporation of this moisture cools the body.
2. *Radiation.* When the body is warmer than the outside temperature, heat leaves the body in particles or waves. (When outside air is warmer, heat radiates into our bodies.)
3. *Conduction.* Body heat flows into objects in actual contact with the body (clothing, air, or water). In a very cold environment, air and water are the most dangerous conductors.
4. *Convection.* Moving air (the wind, for example) transports heat away from the body.

The body loses heat through all four means. Since all bodies lose heat in cold environments, insulation with proper clothing and shelter are crucial. If the body is wet, or has bare skin exposed to the wind and cold, heat is lost at a very rapid rate.

The first priority in a cold, wet and windy survival situation is to *get out of the wind*—it can kill you. Second, *stay dry.*

Wool clothing can help in wet conditions as it is still about 40% effective when wet. Synthetic fibers (Hollofill, Dac II, Thinsulite, etc.) also maintain warmth. Other types of clothing lose up to 90% of their insulative value when wet.

Don't flounder around in the snow or rain any more than necessary, and try not to work up a sweat.

When hiking alone, if you start shivering (the first sign of hypothermia), *stop!* You may be unable to recognize further signs of hypothermia. Build a fire and get out of the bone-chilling rain, the soggy wet clothes, the wind—whatever is causing the heat loss. Get warmed up. Sit out the weather until you can travel safely.

Every group should have a leader. Even if there are just three people one should be the leader, and he's responsible to check the group for signs of hypothermia. He makes the decision when the group should stop, make camp, and get warm. The leader also needs to be watched.

If it's cold, wear a hat. An uncovered head can account for up to eighty percent of a person's heat loss in cold weather. Other important heat loss areas are the knees, the wrists, and the throat or neck area. They are heat regulator areas. The best protection is to cover the head and get on dry, long-legged pants, a long-sleeved shirt, and a bandanna, scarf, or something to tie around your neck.

In addition to clothing, food intake and energy output control body temperature. If really exhausted (you got up in the morning, ate a light breakfast, and spent the day climbing and hiking in the mountains), the chances for hypothermia are greatly increased.

Eating snow is a common mistake many people make, and is one sure way to lose body heat. It not only requires body heat to melt the snow, but it cools the body from the inside, cooling the vital organs in the body core.

If inactive, cold and losing heat, do exercises. This will increase blood circulation and body heat. Stop these exercises before starting to perspire, as the sweating process is a cooling system. The exercises provide some heat for your body, but also increases the body's need for food. If you don't have anything to eat it might be better to limit exercise.

Double-check to make sure heat is not being lost through radiation, conduction, or convection, and be sure you are sheltered from the wind and wet, and insulated from the cold.

Heat

When stranded in the desert or in hot weather the primary concern is getting out of the sun. Find shelter—a tree, some bushes, a rock overhang—anything for shade as long as it is nearby. If you try to cover much distance in the heat you probably won't make it.

You will dehydrate, but how long it will take depends on how much water is in you. If you do any kind of work or any strenuous hiking without really being saturated with water, you'll dehydrate in a couple of hours and be in real trouble. For the immediate 24-hour period, you can get by without a drink *if* you can get in the shade. Nothing else you can do is more important.

If you have a car and there is no natural source of shade, get in or get under it. Two or three layers of insulation from the sun are better than one.

If waiting in your car, leave the doors open. The air will be stale and motionless but tolerable. Don't forget to disconnect the interior lights and do not play the car radio, air conditioner, or use any other car accessories that will draw current from the battery. (When it's cooled off and time to dig out, or change the tire, you don't want to be stuck with a dead battery.)

Minimize the amount of work you do; the same goes for hiking. Limit hiking in the heat of the day to no more than 500 yards. Does this sound exaggerated? In 120 degrees, a one-mile hike would be like running in place for twenty minutes in a sauna. This is why any repairs to your vehicle requiring physical exertion (such as digging your vehicle out of the sand) should be postponed until late afternoon or evening when the temperature drops.

Under the car the sand will be hot until it's been in the shade for awhile. Get your shovel out (or a knife, hubcap, piece of mirror—anything) and dig some sand out, two to five inches.

The deeper you go, the cooler the sand will be, and more tolerable to lie in.

Stay away from the engine, muffler, and transmission; they'll be giving off a lot of heat. If a blanket is in the car, or something similar, drape it over the shady side of the car, making a kind of tent. This will keep shade longer than if you were just under the car.

Do not, under any circumstance, remove all of your clothes! You may feel more comfortable in the heat without clothes on, because the sweat evaporates more rapidly; but it will cause you to lose more water and dehydrate. Any part of the body exposed to the sun's ultraviolet rays for any length of time will burn severely in a matter of hours or less.

Don't remove any of your clothes except clothing that will not allow the body to breathe like a heavy leather jacket. Don't discard anything where you can't find it. The temperature may become very cool at night.

Water intake is vitally important in helping the body ward off heat disease (heat cramps, heat exhaustion, or heat stroke). As long as the body contains enough water to enable it to perspire, it is able to maintain a normal internal temperature. When heat cannot be dissipated into the environment, and builds up inside the body, heat disease is the result.

If you're hiking and start to perspire, take off your hat, roll up your sleeves so your wrists are exposed, and undo your collar so your throat is exposed. These are the thermostat areas of your body, and sometimes by uncovering them to air, you can keep from having to stop and shed clothing.

If you don't perspire easily and you become overheated quickly, find shade and remain there until you cool off. Keep drinking water and dunk your head every time you come to water. It might be beneficial to wet your bandanna and then tie it around your neck to cause a greater heat loss in this critical area, or to wet your shirt.

Wilderness Medicine

Cold Diseases

Hypothermia

Shivering is the first sign the body is trying to produce heat. The shivering itself is a method the body uses to create body heat to replace lost heat. If you're shivering, your body is losing heat. Whatever you're using or doing to keep warm it isn't working.

Cessation of shivering indicates that the body has expended its supply of sugar and protein needed to make heat. It has "given up," and quit shivering.

Stiffness of movement is another symptom. Perhaps you've experienced this before. We've had our hands get so stiff we couldn't untie ropes, or barely tie our shoes. The body has pulled all the heat from the extremities into the core.

Lack of coordination: The victim is unable to walk. He'll stumble, due to the stiffness of his body, and because his brain has quit functioning clearly.

Bluish, clammy, cold skin (similar to the symptoms of shock) is another symptom. Again, the body has pulled all of its heat into the core.

Plodding straight ahead is a sign of a more advanced stage of hypothermia. The person doesn't notice anything, not even where he's going. He just marches down the trail. Yell at him and he responds slowly, if at all. His speech is slow and slurred. The victim forgets. He stops to take a rest, removes his gloves or hat (perhaps even throws them away), and when he leaves, doesn't put them back on. He may unbutton his coat and not do it back up. Again, these are symptoms of advanced hypothermia.

Refusal to move is a critical sign. The victim sits down, not caring whether he lives or dies. He tells you to go on, he'll be okay. Movements are now extremely uncoordinated. He may even go into spastic movements, pawing at you with stiff hands and arms.

Convulsions: Finally the victim may go into convulsions and die. Generally in convulsions there is a foaming at the mouth, along with the other usual symptoms of convulsions.

Temperature: Checking someone's temperature to make sure he is really in hypothermia, and to gauge how far along he is, might be helpful. A rectal temperature reading is necessary. Once the heat is drawn into the body core, an oral temperature may not give an accurate reading. Start treatment at any temperature below 95 degrees; any reading below 90 degrees will require immediate treatment. Below 80 degrees, the chances of surviving are almost zero.

Hypothermia

Rectal Temperatures

99 - 96 degrees	—Uncontrollable and extreme shivering; lack ability to perform complex tasks.
95 - 91 degrees	—Continued violent shivering; difficulty in speaking clearly.
90 - 86 degrees	—Decreased shivering, replaced by strong muscular rigidity; dulled thinking, and unclear comprehension of the situation; erratic or jerky movements due to loss of muscle coordination.
85 - 81 degrees	—Irrational and dazed behavior; respiration and pulse slow; continued muscle rigidity.
80 - 78 degrees	—Unconsciousness; irregular heartbeat; cessation of most reflexes.
Below 78 degrees	—Non-function of the respiratory and cardiac control centers of the brain, causing cardiac fibrillation, and probably hemorrhage and edema in the lungs; death.

Treatment: Try to get something warm inside the victim, like hot soup or even hot water. This may be impossible if the victim can't swallow without choking, or if he's unconscious.

Get the victim to an outside heat source to help warm him. Putting him into a sleeping bag or covering him with blankets or clothing is not enough. He will probably still die. Once the body core temperature reaches 90 degrees, it's a downhill run. The body can no longer build its own heat. If a shelter, fire or warm house isn't available, create the heat for the victim yourself. If you do have a warm house, get him in it. Put the victim in a warm tub of water and, if conscious, get warm liquids inside him. Use an electric blanket or anything possible to give him some heat.

If out in the wilderness, carefully build fires on both sides of the victim, but not too close. He probably can't tell you if you're burning him. Put warm bedding under him and place reflectors behind the fires to create an area of heat around him.

Another method is to take the victim's clothing off, then put him in a sleeping bag with someone's warm body right next to him. Even better is two bodies, one on each side, without clothing. This allows the direct contact of the body heat. Warm stones or bottles with warm water can also be used as a heat source. As soon as possible, get something warm inside the victim so his body can start working from the inside to produce heat.

If possible, it is recommended the rapid rewarming from the outside should be done under the direction of a physician in a medical facility. There is a chance it may increase shock by increasing circulation to the skin and extremities, and the core temperature may continue to fall after outside warming has begun. Judgment must be used. If he must be rewarmed where he is, then do it without moving him.

A victim in the advanced stages of hypothermia may appear dead. He may have very light heart action, the heart sounds may not be audible and the pulse may not be felt. If this is the case, but there is any doubt, begin CPR along with the rewarming. Although cases have lived when thought dead, the key is fast action in the early stages to insure success.

Jarring a person in advance stages of hypothermia may cause cardiac arrest. The victim must be transported with extreme care and be monitored for pulse and breathing constantly.

Do not, under any circumstances, give whiskey or other alcoholic drinks. It's often the first thing people want to give someone who is cold, but it is a depressant that constricts the capillaries and slows down the circulation, adding to the problem.

On the trail, use warm powdered milk and brown sugar, which is excellent for someone suffering from hypothermia. Hot broth is also good.

If you want to learn more about hypothermia, two excellent movies are available: "By Nature's Rules," put out by the Mountain Rescue Association; and "Hypothermia—Enemy Number One," put out by Life Support Technology, in Oregon.

Frostbite

Frostbite can occur anytime the temperature is below 32 degrees. In most cases it occurs at zero and below.

Wind chill is an important factor in frostbite because wind alters the temperature very quickly. If the temperature is ten degrees above zero and there is a 20 mile-per-hour wind, the wind chill factor is 25 degrees below zero. When the temperature is this low, flesh can freeze in one minute. If any part of the body is uncovered, it can easily get frostbite.

The most common cases of frostbite today are linked to snowmobiling. When snowmobiling on a beautiful, sunshiny day, with temperatures at 15 - 20 degrees F., and traveling 40 - 50 miles per hour, the equivalent chill temperature is minus 30 degrees. In these conditions, an exposed face can easily get frostbite.

Anytime temperatures drop into the "danger degrees" (temperatures below minus 25 degrees F., figuring wind chill), cover all exposed flesh or take a chance of frostbite! In exceptionally cold temperatures, cover all exposed flesh extremely well.

A man in Alaska, out in − 70 degree weather (figuring the wind chill), had on good foot gear, but the skin ten inches above his boot was a series of blisters because his long johns and pants weren't enough protection. Another man froze his fingers because he took his glove off and screwed a burr onto a bolt in − 40 degrees. He blistered his fingertips in 30 seconds.

Few people venture out in − 40 to − 70 degree weather, but many forget the wind chill factor.

Symptoms: The areas of the body which are usually frostbitten are the extremities—the fingers, nose, ears, and toes.

TEMPERATURE AND WIND CHILL CHART

Cooling Power of Wind Expressed as "Equivalent Chill Temperature"

Wind Speed Knots	MPH	Temperature (°F) Calm	40	35	30	25	20	15	10	5	0	-5	-10	-15	-20	-25	-30	-35	-40	-45	-50	-55	-60
Calm	Calm		40	35	30	25	20	15	10	5	0	-5	-10	-15	-20	-25	-30	-35	-40	-45	-50	-55	-60
3-6	5		35	30	25	20	15	10	5	0	-5	-10	-15	-20	-25	-30	-35	-40	-45	-50	-55	-65	-70
7-10	10		30	20	15	10	5	0	-10	-15	-20	-25	-35	-40	-45	-50	-60	-65	-70	-75	-80	-90	-95
11-15	15		25	15	10	0	-5	-10	-20	-25	-30	-40	-45	-50	-60	-65	-70	-80	-85	-90	-100	-105	-110
16-19	20		20	10	5	0	-10	-15	-25	-30	-35	-45	-50	-60	-65	-75	-80	-85	-95	-100	-110	-115	-120
20-23	25		15	10	0	-5	-15	-20	-30	-35	-45	-50	-60	-65	-75	-80	-90	-95	-105	-110	-120	-125	-135
24-28	30		10	5	0	-10	-20	-25	-30	-40	-50	-55	-65	-70	-80	-85	-95	-100	-110	-115	-125	-130	-140
29-32	35		10	5	-5	-10	-20	-30	-35	-40	-50	-60	-65	-75	-80	-90	-100	-105	-115	-120	-130	-135	-145
33-36	40		10	0	-5	-15	-20	-30	-35	-45	-55	-60	-70	-75	-85	-95	-100	-110	-115	-125	-130	-140	-150

Winds above 40 have little additional effect

Equivalent Chill Temperature

Little Danger

Increasing Danger (Flesh may freeze within one minute)

Great Danger (Flesh may freeze within thirty seconds)

There is first, second, and third degree frostbite, similar to first, second, and third degree burns.

First degree frostbite is the most common. The flesh turns a whitish or bluish color, is waxy or frosty looking, and fairly pliable. The fingers will be stiff and numb, but won't be frozen solid. After the area is warmed, the skin may peel off, or a few small blisters may form.

Second degree frostbite involves skin damage and some tissue damage. The flesh becomes a bit mushy, like half-frozen ice cream—white and waxy. When thawed, it blisters and often turns black. The skin may all come off.

Third degree frostbite causes the entire appendage to freeze solid. Extreme caution is necessary. The frozen parts may break off, as they are brittle! After thawing, the skin blisters severely. In third degree frostbite (sometimes even in second degree), it's quite possible to lose the appendage.

Treatment: The best treatment for frostbite is to discover it quickly before it has a chance to do much damage. When riding on snowmobiles, skiing, snow shoeing or just playing in minus zero degree weather, habitually check every three to five minutes for frostbite by crinkling up faces and wiggling toes. If a numb area is discovered, stop right then, thaw the area and cover it to protect it from further frostbite.

The best way to thaw minor frostbitten appendages is in 105° to 110°F. water. The victim must be in a place where his entire body can stay warm before the frozen area is thawed out, as there must be a good blood supply to the area after it is thawed. If he is cold, there will not be an adequate blood supply.

Rapid rewarming is a must, but water over 110° should not be used, as further tissue damage will result. Rewarming should be continued for at least thirty minutes even though there is great pain. Aspirin and codeine can be given.

In the wilderness, where warm water is not available, use armpits, stomach, or crotch to thaw hands. If feet are frostbitten, use someone's chest or stomach, or put your feet between their thighs. Using a fire is dangerous. A frozen appendage is numb and could literally be burned without ever feeling it!

Do not, under any circumstance, rub the frostbitten area with snow. This "old wives' tale" should be put to rest. Never massage a frostbitten area with snow or even warm hands. If you do, you risk further tissue damage.

To start circulation in a frozen appendage, move it up and down. This will help restore circulation without causing further tissue damage.

Avoid drinking alcohol. It burns carbohydrates, causing a loss of body heat. Also avoid using tobacco, as it constricts the blood vessels, thus limiting the flow of blood and body heat to the frostbitten area, which promotes infection.

Once the frostbitten area is thawed, bandage it loosely (it's going to swell) with a sterile dry bandage.

An actual frozen appendage (third degree frostbite) is another matter. If a victim is out in the wilderness with frozen hands or feet, and there is another day to go before reaching any medical aid, *don't* thaw them out! Leave them frozen. If a frozen appendage is thawed and refreezes, it causes an automatic case of gangrene! There can be no trauma or use of a frozen area immediately after it is thawed. If his feet are frozen, once thawed they will be swollen and painful, and he'll be unable to walk. It's possible to walk a full day on frozen feet and not do any more damage than has already been done, but once a victim's feet are thawed, he'll probably be unable to walk on them for at least six weeks and, depending on the severity of the case, he may lose them altogether.

Get the victim to a medical facility, and to a doctor. Frostbite (especially second and third degree) is very serious and should be treated by a professional. Check at the hospital to see if someone is qualified (someone with experience) to handle frostbite. A decision to amputate should not be made for at least three weeks, even though the frostbitten areas turn completely black, shrivel up, and look like they're going to fall off. After three to six weeks, life can come back. Doctors generally wait at least that long before resorting to amputation. If after three to six weeks the appendages are still dead, they must be surgically removed.

Once frozen, an area becomes especially susceptible to refreezing forever as there is permanent damage to the blood vessels.

Heat Diseases

It takes about one week to acclimatize to heat. Lack of this acclimatization, and/or salt deficiency, and/or dehydration help to bring on heat disease.

Heat Cramps

Heat cramps, the mildest form of heat disease, are generally caused by heavy perspiring due to strenuous activity in high heat and humidity. Because of the excessive perspiration, the salt level in the blood and tissues is depleted. Heat cramps can also be caused by drinking ice water or other drinks in too great a quantity.

Symptoms are cramps in the legs and abdomen, along with intermittant muscle spasms. The pupils may dilate with each spasm. The body temperature remains normal.

Treatment is to rest and replace lost salt by sipping salt water (one teaspoon per quart of water), by taking salt tablets accompanied by plenty of water (not more than two tablets per quart of water), or by sucking a perspiration-soaked article of clothing. Cramped muscles should be massaged. A victim usually recovers very quickly after salt intake.

Heat Exhaustion

Heat exhaustion is usually caused from exercise and heavy perspiring, not from actual heat. Hiking uphill in heavy clothes can cause both heat exhaustion and heat cramps.

Symptoms of heat exhaustion are headache, dizziness, drowsiness, confusion, low blood pressure, possible vomiting, and physical weakness much the same as dehydration. The skin is pale and sweaty, and the skin temperature is cool or near normal.

Treat by keeping the victim prone, and slightly elevating his feet. Replace the lost salt and water (give a saline solution— ½ tsp. soda and 1 tsp. salt per quart of water) if the victim is conscious. Keep the victim in the shade, and as cool as possible. The victim may be cooled by wetting the head and clothing.

Heat Stroke or Sunstroke

Heat stroke or sunstroke is the opposite of hypothermia. The body overheats, disabling the heat regulator in the brain, and is unable to get rid of the excess body heat.

Symptoms: In heat stroke the skin flushes or turns pink, then becomes purple or ashen; the skin is usually dry and hot. The body suddenly collapses because it is overheated.

Heat stroke usually comes on very rapidly. The victim, after heavy sweating, ceases to sweat and becomes confused and uncoordinated, slipping into delirium and/or unconsciousness.

The key to diagnosis is that the victim's temperature is 105° or above, there is no sweating, and the skin is hot and dry to touch. Unconsciousness can result and is not uncommon. This is brought about by blood vessels becoming so dilated, to help cool the body, that inadequate supplies reach the brain.

Many people who suffer from heat stroke are dehydrated before starting physical activity that results in this disease. Both antihistamines and belladonna products (for digestive disturbances) limit body perspiration and can provoke heat stroke. The obese, old and very young seem to be the most susceptible.

Treatment: This is a true medical emergency and treatment must be immediate. The body must be cooled. Treatment should start if the body temperature is over 102 degrees. The limbs should be massaged all during the cooling to keep the circulation moving in the extremities and to speed up cooling of vital organs. This is important. No aspirin should be given.

The biggest heat loss will be through the head, so a good treatment is to dunk the victim's head (keep the face up) in a stream, if one is nearby. If the water is icy cold, don't leave the head in very long. If plenty of water is available, immerse the entire body, clothes and all. bandannas or clothing can be rotated on the head and neck area of the victim.

The cold water will be quite a shock to the victim's system. Some students have screamed and cried because they didn't want to go in, but this is the only way to quickly cool them off. After taking them out they sometimes start to shiver and shake violently, but that is not a problem. Heat loss is taking place, and that's good.

Dunking a victim in a river or creek for heat stroke should bring relief rather quickly. In a relapse, the procedure should be repeated.

The cooling can be stopped when the victim's temperature drops to 102°F., but if the victim starts to heat again, resume cooling.

If the victim stays in a coma after cooling, they must be evacuated as soon as possible. They probably have brain damage from the high fever.

If the unconsciousness and high fever are brief, recovery is usually quite rapid. Untreated sun stroke is always fatal. Damage in sun stroke victims is directly related to the amount of time lapsed before treatment was started.

Anyone recovering from heat stroke can expect to have trouble with heat in the future and should be careful.

Fevers

If somebody has a high fever on the trail, and you can't bring the fever down, dunking him in cool water will generally help break the fever.

General Information

While reducing a victim's body temperature externally, give him a mixture of one teaspoon of salt or two salt tablets to a quart of water, and let him drink it slowly. He should drink at least four ounces every 15 minutes. It's better if this water is just a little bit warm. The victim's system is so overheated that cold water probably won't stay down.

On the trail we encounter a combination of heat-caused problems. The students we've treated had flushed faces and headaches, were physically weak and sometimes had abdominal cramps. Occasionally they were dizzy. They had usually quit sweating, or weren't sweating very heavily.

One way to avoid heat exhaustion, cramps, or stroke is to take salt pills before going out, or during the time spent hiking, drink lots of water, and if you start getting hot, stop and cool off. Use salt tablets sparingly. Never take more than one tablet per quart of water unless treating heat disease. If salt tablets are taken without adequate water, the concentration of salt increases in the stomach and the intestines. The body then withdraws water from the blood into the intestines, making less water available for perspiring and actually reducing the body's ability to cool itself.

Up to 80% of your body heat is concentrated in the head, so always keep your head shaded. Wear a wide-brim hat.

Along with a good hat, a scarf is also handy for covering the back and sides of the neck. The neck is a critical area for two reasons; (1) the back of your neck (the base of the brain) is the location of the body's thermostat, and (2) the sides of the neck contain arteries close to the skin's surface. These arteries carry blood to the brain, and if the neck surface absorbs excessive amounts of heat, the blood going to the brain may also be heated to a critical level, with sunstroke being the end result.

Dehydration

Dehydration develops both when it's cold and when it's hot; perhaps more easily in the cold because you don't develop a thirst, but it certainly is more common in the heat of summer. Diarrhea also contributes significantly to dehydration, so always carry diarrhea pills in your first aid kit, and drink whenever water is available.

Symptoms: The first signs of dehydration, being vague, are commonly overlooked: loss of appetite, nausea, drowsiness, general discomfort, and a lack of desire to move around.

The secondary warnings of a water deficiency are a little more noticeable: dizziness, dry mouth, headaches, yellow urine, "rubbery" legs, and difficulty in speech. The yellow urine is probably the first noticeable sign. Even in the secondary stage of dehydration, you may not feel thirsty.

The third-stage warnings of dehydration are the need to lie down, strange speech, perhaps spasms, swollen tongue, sore mouth and throat; a white, foamy crust around the mouth (the saliva is solidifying), cessation of sweating, and diminished senses. Urine volume over a 24-hour period is a sure way to monitor dehydration. If the output is less than a pint, there is not enough fluid intake.

These are the main stages of dehydration; but it is very likely many of these symptoms will not be noticeable. Therefore, it is important to take action if any of the symptoms occur.

Treatment: Dehydration should be treated with water, salt, and shade, but don't take salt unless you have plenty of water to accompany it, and don't eat food unless there is plenty of water. Food is not necessary, water is; and taking in food will only increase your need for water.

Sunburn

To guard against sunburn, keep clothes on, wear a hat, and don't expose the skin to sunlight. Most people link sunburn to summer, but you can get sunburned in the winter just as easily. People who take their shirts off on a warm, sunny day out on the snow burn fast, especially at high altitudes, because of the reflection off the snow.

A severe sunburn may prove disastrous. A second degree burn blisters the skin, and runs a high risk of infection, plus loss of body fluid.

Sunscreen products provide effective protection from sunburn and windburn. The most effective sunscreens contain either PABA, cinnamates, homosalicylate, anthranillate, or benzophenones.

Treatment: Cover the burned areas to protect from further exposure. If possible, cool with water and apply topical anesthetic spray or ointment to relieve pain. It is important to draw the heat out of the skin so don't use lotion or ointment with a paraffin or oil base. Vinegar helps mild sunburn if nothing else is available. The barks of pine, hemlock, chestnut, oak or elderberry leaves can be boiled in water and the concentrated solution used on blistered sunburns. Severe sunburns with open blisters should be treated by a physician.

Snow/Sun Blindness

A person should not go out in the winter without some kind of sun glasses or tinted goggles for prevention of snow blindness. If you wear regular glasses, the polaroid clip-ons are excellent. In the summer, direct or reflected sunlight can burn your eyes, but snowblindness is most common.

In an emergency improvise a makeshift covering for your eyes by using a bandanna, handkerchief, or some article of clothing. Tie the bandanna over your face and cut a small slit for each eye, or use adhesive tape, leaving thin slits, over your regular glasses. Some stocking caps can be pulled down over your face and still allow vision. You can also darken around your eyes with charcoal, but to be 100% safe, you need something to cut out the sun's ultraviolet rays.

Even on overcast, cloudy days, you can still be snow blinded. Blue-eyed people are more susceptible to it than dark-eyed people, but anyone can become snow blind.

Symptoms: Symptoms may not begin to appear for eight to twelve hours after exposure. The eyes will feel scratchy and

full of sand. They burn, water and sight may become hazy—
mostly a blur of light and dark things. Eyes will appear to be
bloodshot. If protection is not provided the eyes will get extremely painful.

Treatment: If you do get snow blindness, put a bandage
over both eyes to block out *all* light. Any light will increase the
burning and watering of your inflamed eyes, and also cause
headaches or extremely poor vision.

It will be from one day to one week, generally about three
to five days, before you'll be able to use your eyes again. Cold
compresses and aspirin may alleviate the pain.

A product called Holocaine HC-1, cortisone or some other
steroid ophtalmic ointment can be used to treat eyes. The
deadeners ease the pain and enable you to use your eyes after
a day or two; however, it can soften the cornea and may allow
infections, so it is not suggested except in emergency situations.

Altitude Sickness

The condition commonly called altitude sickness is
brought about by a lower oxygen concentration in the blood
due to the lower atmospheric pressure at higher altitudes.

Acclimatization is the only sure way to avoid altitude
problems. It takes from six to ten days to reach 80% acclimatization. The body begins to be affected at 3,000 feet above sea
level and the effects increase as the altitude increases.

The most effective method of acclimatizing is moving up
500 to 1,000 feet per day, with an occasional rest day in between
and no heavy exercise output.

Physical condition plays no role in preventing altitude
problems, nor do any drugs or vitamins; but there is evidence
that persons over 25 years of age have less problems with
altitude.

The most common altitude problem is called Acute Mountain Sickness. It covers a variety of symptoms and problems.
The symptoms generally will begin within a few hours of the
rise in elevation. By the third day the symptoms generally
begin to decrease.

Symptoms for some individuals begin at 8,000 to 10,000
feet in elevation. Most people have symptoms at 14,000 feet.

Symptoms are fatigue, headache, dizziness, shortness of breath, nausea and vomiting along with loss of appetite. Children seem more prone to nausea and vomiting. Drowsiness and yawning along with disturbed sleep are common. The general feeling of suffering a hangover or the flu are quite often present.

More common at altitudes above 14,000 are symptoms which indicate Cerebral Altitude Sickness.

Symptoms are memory loss, headache, confusion, dizziness and a slowdown of mental acuity. If the condition becomes severe, there may be nerve paralysis, hallucinations, psychotic behavior or coma.

Treatment: People with altitude sickness should avoid tobacco, alcohol and heavy exertion; however, they should engage in light outdoor activities rather than complete rest. Extra fluid intake and a light high-carbohydrate diet are also helpful. A treatment being tested with good results reported is to use an antiacid (like Rolaids) to keep the urine pH at 5.5 to 6.5 The pH is checked with pH test paper on the urine. This is used with drinking enough fluids to maintain a urinary output of 1.0 to 1.5 quarts per 24 hours. If climbing, eat 3 ounces of a high-carbohydrate every hour. Aspirin may be used for headaches but sedatives or any drug that reduces respiration should be avoided. In all high altitude problems, recovery should be rapid if descent of 2,000 to 3,000 feet in elevation is made.

Edema often occurs at high altitudes and is a harmless disorder. It should go away upon returning to lower altitudes. It may be more common in women during their premenstrual periods.

The disorder called *High Altitude Pulmonary Edema* is the *most dangerous* of common altitude sicknesses. The causes of this disorder are not fully understood. The results are air sacs in the lungs filling with fluid. This ultimately brings on suffocation. This can occur at elevations as low as 8,000 feet and, once in a great while, at even lower elevations. The most common occurance is with individuals completing a rapid ascent to higher altitudes and not acclimatizing, then performing heavy physical exercise after arrival at the high altitudes. Children and adolescents appear to be more susceptible to this problem.

Symptoms begin one to four days after arrival at the high altitude. They consist of shortness of breath and a feeling of suffocation, especially at night. In addition, the victim may have a headache, nausea and vomiting and is more tired than other members of the party. The first important sign is a dry cough. The cough will develop into a persistent cough, with white frothy or watery sputum which may become streaked with blood. Breathing is rapid (20 to 40 breaths per minute), and pulse is usually very rapid (110 to 160 per minute, even after rest). Lips and nails often have a blue tinge, and a crackling or gurgling sound may be heard in the chest. At night the symptoms become worse.

The level of severity in this disorder can be judged by the oxygen supply to the brain. The less oxygen, the more delirium, confusion and irrational behavior occurs. If the individual goes into a coma or unconsciousness, death may be just two to six hours away.

Treatment: The number-one treatment is to drop 2,000 to 3,000 feet in elevation and if oxygen is available, administer it immediately at 4 liters per minute for the first fifteen minutes, then two liters per minute with a snug-fitting face mask. It should be given at least six to twelve hours before they are moved down. They must be moved down and, once down, given complete rest. Once the condition starts, the individual must not exert himself.

Prevention for all high altitude sicknesses is gradual ascent and acclimatization. If you must do a rapid ascent, it should be followed by rest and minimal physical exertion the first few days after arrival at the high altitude. Acclimatization is lost in 6 to 10 days after return to lower elevations.

Basic First Aid

In any medical emergency, always check first for bleeding, breathing, heartbeat, and shock. If you don't know how to deal with these emergencies, take a course in first aid before getting involved in much extensive outdoor activity. You should also know how to splint broken bones and treat burns and infections.

Closing a Wound: An important first aid technique is "butterfly stitching." It can be used on any wound that would normally receive sutures, or any wound that would probably leave a scar unless otherwise attended.

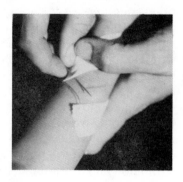

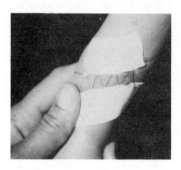

Fold 1/8" on adhesive side of 1" wide cloth tape. Place folded edge 3/4" from laceration. Sew through the folded edge of tape, pulling the cut together. Use only on lacerations no more then skin deep, except on temporary basis until medical help. Put antibacterial salve on cut. Leave "stitches" 5 days.

Butterfly Stitching

Butterfly stitching or steri-stripping (a commercial product used to close wounds) is recommended rather than waiting to get to a doctor. If it's been over eight hours since the injury, a doctor won't suture a laceration. Stitching a cut after eight hours increases the chance of infection by about 50%. It's far better to care for a wound with a butterfly stitch or steri-strips when it happens, and everything is clean.

Once a dressing is applied, keep clean. Change the dressing daily and put on more salve if needed. The biggest risk with an open cut is infection, so watch it closely. The following is a basic list of major problems and treatments, but in no way is it a substitute for a good first aid course:

Bleeding:

Apply direct pressure to the wound.

Elevate the injury, if possible.

If an artery has been severed, apply pressure to the nearest pressure point (first aid training advised).

Use a tourniquet as a last resort with the understanding that the victim may possibly lose that limb.

Breathing:

First check for any obstruction in the air passage.

Give mouth-to-mouth resuscitation.

Heartbeat:

Check for pulse, preferably at the neck, not the wrist.

Start CPR heart massage. (You must have training.)

Shock:

Keep the victim lying down and warm (covered).

If possible, elevate the feet slightly—but not if the victim is having trouble breathing, or has a chest injury.

Give a saline solution if the victim is conscious (1/8 tsp. soda and 1/4 tsp. salt per 8 ounces water).

Burns:

Immerse the burn in cold water or apply ice until the heat is pulled out.

Then cover the area with several layers of soft, wet cloth; cover that with plastic, sealing the edges down.

Give a saline solution if the victim is conscious.

Splinting:

Immobilize the break area and both adjoining joints.

Do not tie the splint too tightly, since the limb will swell. Check the circulation every 10 to 20 minutes.

When in doubt about a break, splint it.

If a broken back or neck is suspected, the victim must be kept absolutely flat.

Medicinal and Other Useful Plants

In the wilderness, the ability to identify and use the common plants is a great asset, because plants can be used for a variety of purposes other than food. Here are some common plants and their uses.

Heartleaf arnica, which grows in lodgepole pine forest areas, can be used to aid healing and prevent infection in open cuts or sores. Make a poultice out of the crushed petals of the flower, put it right on the cut, and then bandage. If there are no flowers, use the leaves. Crushed *plantain* leaves will also work for healing cuts. *Yarrow* will work to a degree.

Wild onion or *yarrow* is your best bet as an insect repellent. Crush and rub the plant on your skin. In heavy insect areas it is good for about 30 minutes, then has to be renewed.

Any kind of *mint* or *yarrow* works well for an upset stomach. Make a tea by steeping the leaves, then drink it slowly until the stomach has settled. *Catnip* tea both settles an upset stomach and relieves gas cramps.

Use any part of the *willow* as an aspirin replacement for headache, fever, pain, etc. Make a tea and drink it. It isn't nearly as strong as aspirin, so drink quite a bit. The white powder on the outer bark of the *quaking aspen* tree will also work as aspirin. Again make a tea (1 teaspoon of powder to a cup of water). Both willow and quaking aspen bark contain "salicin" which is found in aspirin.

The inner bark on any species of *pine* tree (particularly white pine) acts as a disinfectant when it's boiled, for cuts, burns, and other wounds. It can also be boiled, mashed, and used as a dressing right over a cut or open sore. Use the inner bark of a *pine* tree to make a disinfectant to treat the burn area.

Once a burn is disinfected, further treat it by applying a rather runny salve made from the bark of the *pine, chestnut, hemlock, or oak;* or the leaves of *elderberry.* All of these act as astringents and inhibit the release of body fluids to the burn area.

If poison ivy, poison oak, or poison sumac, is the problem, gather *elderberry* leaves, the inner bark of a *pine* tree, or the bark of *oak,* and boil down to a salve to put on your rash. You can make a tea and use it on your skin, but *do not* drink it!

Cool mud on stinging nettle will take the sting away.

You can use *yucca* root, *snowberry,* or *snow bush* flowers or leaves to make soap. Peel, then pound the yucca root, while wetting it with water to bring out the soap. With snowberry and snow bush, crush the flowers or leaves, wet the area to be washed, and rub the crushed flowers or leaves on the area. None of these will lather like commercial products, but they work well as cleaning agents. The *yucca* is especially good shampoo. You can also mix ashes, water, and animal fat to make a good lye soap for washing poison ivy or poison oak.

To make cordage (for securing dressings, splinting, etc.), *stinging nettle, milkweed, sagebrush bark, juniper bark, cliff rose bark, and dogbane* (which is very poisonous) are the best fiber plants. *White clematis, willow bark, wild grape bark,* and the inner bark on old *cottonwood* trees that have fallen down can also be used for cordage, but they are not as strong. *Spruce roots* and young *willows,* when fresh and wet, can be used to tie things; however, both become brittle when dry.

Left to right: (Top) Stinging nettle, bitter brush, willow bark, sagebrush bark. (Bottom) Juniper bark, bunch grass, dogbane, milkweed.

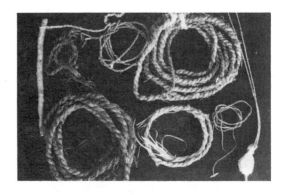

Nature's Cordage

3

Shelters and Keeping Warm

Campsite Selection

When choosing a campsite, look for the warmest, most sheltered area you can find—one with plenty of wood and water. It should be about halfway up a slope. It should never be in the bottom of a canyon. Quite often, the ridge on top will be warmer than the bottom, if you can get out of the wind. Cold air settles into a canyon during the night, making temperatures ten to fifteen degrees cooler.

Find a campsite away from the creek, up high. Do your sleeping up there, and your cooking and eating down by the creek.

Quite often the mosquitoes and gnats will be fewer on top of a ridge, especially where there's a light breeze blowing. If you can get somewhat out of the wind to sleep, you will still be warmer, and the wind will keep the flying insects away. If unable to find a place to get away from the mosquitoes, and you have no repellent, build a smudge fire and sleep in the smoke all night.

Be careful not to pick a campsite near an ant bed, or where there are visible signs of ants. We've had our worst problems with insects when we had to pick our campsite after dark, or sleep under logs when nothing else was available. We've never slept underneath a log without having insects crawling on us all night.

Unless you're carrying a little backpack stove, pick an area with plenty of firewood. These stoves are essential in areas where wood is scarce.

It is warmer to sleep at least one-third up the slope.

Cold air settles in the bottom by the creek.

A wind break should be made against the cold air coming down the slope and down the canyon at night.

In addition to choosing an area with plenty of firewood and water, look for an area that offers some degree of shelter or protection from the wind. Even if there isn't a wind, there will be evening breezes. The cold air drifts down the slopes of a mountain and down a canyon, so find or put up a windbreak. Even if you have a warm sleeping bag, a windbreak of some sort will generally add to your comfort. Just getting behind a log or a large rock will help.

Once in awhile you can't find anything to break the down-slope breezes. In this case, put the fire above you. Then the breezes hit the fire and blow the smoke and heat over the top of you (watch the sparks!). In effect, you block the downhill breeze with your fire.

Camp location should be out of stream beds for warmth and to avoid the danger of flash floods. Places void of green vegetation, or with vegetation such as sagebrush, will be the dryest. The grassy meadow areas—any place with a lot of green vegetation—are damp.

In selecting your site, watch for old, dead trees that might fall over, should a wind come up. Check to see if you are at the base of a rock slide or a rock cliff. If a lot of boulders are lying around, fallen from the cliff, or if the cliff is rotten, you have chosen a dangerous campsite. If there is a weather-temperature change, rocks may come down on you. In lightning weather, avoid large trees, rock outcrops and ridge tops. They all attract lightning.

Shelters

Snow Cave

The most effective winter shelter is a snow cave. Snow caves generally don't get below 30°F., as snow is an excellent insulator. Even when it's extremely cold outside you can be relatively warm inside, even without much sleeping gear. Probe for trees, brush, or other obstacles before starting to dig the cave. The biggest problem encountered in digging a snow cave is getting wet. If exposed to any warmth, such as body heat, the snow will melt; and working in the humid cave will also cause you to perspire freely.

An advantage of a snow cave (unless you have claustrophobia) is that you don't build it much larger than your body,

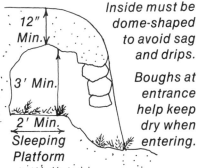

Inside must be dome-shaped to avoid sag and drips.

Boughs at entrance help keep dry when entering.

12" Min.

3' Min.

2' Min.

Sleeping Platform

8' Min.

Top View

Shallow Drift Snow Cave

The doorway is dug as large as needed to avoid getting wet while digging the cave. When cave is finished block up the doorway with chunks of snow. Let set one hour and dig new opening as low as possible below sleeping platform. Place insulation between you and snow.

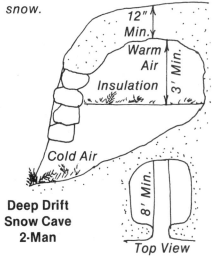

12" Min.

Warm Air

Insulation

3' Min.

Cold Air

Deep Drift Snow Cave 2-Man

8' Min.

Top View

and this small size minimizes the area you have to heat. (it must be large enough to undress and get into sleeping equipment.) A single candle (or candle lantern) is more than sufficient to heat a snow cave. In fact, a candle plus your body heat may prove to be too much, causing some drips or cave sag.

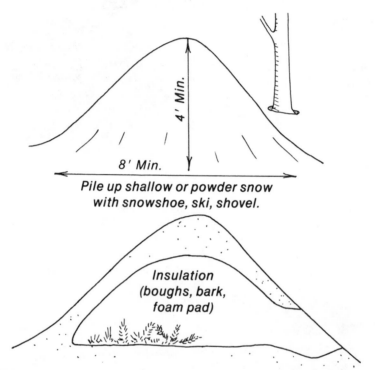

Pile up shallow or powder snow
with snowshoe, ski, shovel.

*Insulation
(boughs, bark,
foam pad)*

*Dig out center; try to place sleeping platform above the door-
way. Make the inside as dome-shaped as possible to avoid
sagging.*

Powder or Shallow Snow Shelter

Some of the dripping problem in snow caves can be elimi-
nated by making the roof of the cave dome-shaped. If your
cave is domed, the snow itself will absorb the moisture. If your
cave is warmer than 32° (which it generally is), the ceiling will
slowly sag. This usually is caused from body heat and gravity.

There is no way to have a regular campfire in a snow cave.
The cave would melt right down around you. In fact, we have
never seen any snow shelter in which you could build a fire.

Snow Trench

Another way to get out of the wind in snow two or more feet deep is to dig a snow trench. As you dig the trench, if possible, cut chunks or blocks of hard-packed snow to form a wall along the side of the trench. This will increase the height of the trench to give you a better wind break. Even if you can't cover the trench, it will get you out of the wind to a large degree. If the choice comes between standing in a − 25 °F. windchill or digging in the snow, start digging! With any luck in snow conditions, you can raise your environment's temperature to 30 °F. or higher.

When snow conditions are good (wind blown and compacted), cut blocks long enough to stand on edge along each side of the trench, leaning them together to form an A-frame roof.

Make the trench walls at least three feet deep, and cover them with pine boughs, branches, sagebrush, etc. The ideal cover is a layer of dead branches of some kind, covered with a layer of spruce or fir boughs, then covered with a foot of snow. Boughs should be about a foot thick over the top before the snow is added; otherwise the snow will filter through.

After climbing in, fill the entrance with snow, your pack, boughs, and whatever. If you manage to seal the entrance air tight, make an air vent somewhere. Once inside, light your candle and settle down for a long winter's nap.

If you're going to be doing much winter camping, practice making snow shelters in your backyard or some other accessible place.

Tree Shelter

In high country where there are spruce trees, quite often you can make a shelter inside the tree near the trunk. Spruce limbs hang down sometimes ten to fifteen feet. Cut out some of the limbs, and you will have access to the area around the trunk—a ready-made house.

This space is not at the base of the tree (very seldom is that space accessible). In spruce country there's generally deep snow (ten to twenty feet), and you can't chop your way through ten feet of limbs to reach the base of the tree. There is no need to dig a hole. Just remain at snow level and chop out

1. *Dig a trench 8' long by 3' wide by 3' deep.*

2. *Place boughs (insulation) in the bottom. Cover with large limbs or poles.*

3. *Cover with boughs, tarp, brush, poncho.*

Entrance must be closed during the night or hot air rises out and cold air settles in the trench.

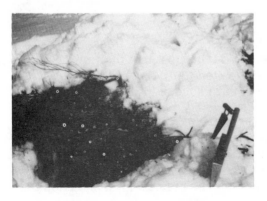

4. *Cover with 12" minimum of snow.*

Snow Trench Shelter

enough limbs to get inside. Then line the floor with the limbs you cut.

This ready-made shelter will protect you from the wind and snow. You can even build a little fire, but be careful. Spruce trees have a lot of pitch, and if you build your fire next to the tree, there's a chance you'll set your house on fire; or if the tree is covered with snow, it will melt and drip on you.

Miscellaneous Shelters

Summer, spring, or fall shelters to provide relief from wind, rain, or cold are slightly more involved than snow shelters. The ability to look around and recognize what is available is your best asset. Try to select the smallest, easiest, and most effective shelter that can be made with the materials available. Some shelters, other than those made from snow, can be used any time of the year.

If you have a tarp or some plastic, you can construct some very simple shelters, not only to protect you from the wind, but also from the rain. If there is no equipment with you, nature can provide. Be inventive: build a shelter from anything you find around you. Illustrations are provided to give you some ideas. Natural shelters like caves, overhangs, hollow logs, etc., are often available, too.

Windbreaks

Anything in sufficient quantity can be used to break the wind. On the Escalante River in southern Utah we used tumble-weeds—big piles that had drifted in the little crannies of the cliffs. We stacked them around, weighed them down with limbs, and enjoyed a good windbreak.

You can also use long, wild grass or weeds by sticking poles in the ground, then stacking the grasses in between them. Use sagebrush, rabbit brush, juniper—anything to create a windbreak. In sand you can dig down, if you can find some way to keep it from drifting on you. Weave cattail plants or willows in between stakes in the ground to make a wall, or stuff the spaces with grass to further insulate you from the wind.

In snow-covered timber country you can build a bough shelter to get out of the wind. Cut the boughs and jam the butt

1.

2.

3.

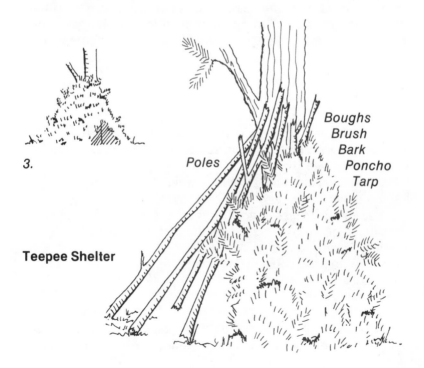

Poles

Boughs
Brush
Bark
Poncho
Tarp

Teepee Shelter

1. Ridge pole with large rock at bottom for anchor.

2. Dead limbs or bark for frame.

3. Cover with tarp, boughs, brush, bark or poncho.

"A" Frame Shelter

Willow & Grass

Douglas Fir Bark

Pole, Forest Debri,
& Dirt

Willow & Juniper Bark

Rock & Firewood Wind Break
with Reflector Fire

Shelter can be
created from
any available
material.

**Lean-to
Shelters**

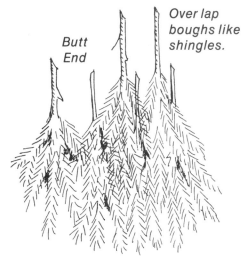

Butt
End

Over lap
boughs like
shingles.

Spruce & Fir boughs make the best covering for shelters. Pine does not shed water.

The boughs should be laid starting at the bottom of the shelter and laying rows overlaping the next row up like shingles, placing the butt end up.

Tarp Shelter

ends (the ends you cut off) vertically into the snow. The boughs can be cut by pulling down on them, and then chopping on top of the pressure point with a large knife. Build a vertical wall a foot thick of overlapped boughs, then get behind it and build a fire in front of you, putting yourself between the wall and the fire. This is a fairly quick way to get out of the wind if the snow is deep enough to support the windbreak.

Boughs, Brush, Bark, Tumbleweeds, Snow Piled, Snow Balls or Snow Blocks

Wind

Insulation: Boughs, Brush, Bark, Foam Pad

Fire Wood

Small fire on log base.

Boughs can be pushed into the snow butt end in with other boughs twined horizontally.

Simple Wind Break

Don't ever cut or use green boughs unless it's an emergency—you're out in a snow storm, a rain storm, or freezing winds! Use them only in a survival situation, not for fun or convenience.

Bedding

It's always warmer if you have some kind of bedding (boughs, grass, etc.) underneath you, even in the summer. A moisture-proof ground cloth keeps you from getting damp. A lot of cold and moisture comes up from the bottom, and seventy percent of your body heat can be lost to the cold surface underneath you.

In all snow shelters, try to put boughs (emergencies only) about a foot thick between your body and the snow. To do this, cut a main limb from a fir or spruce tree (pine doesn't work as well), then cut the little limbs off of the main limb and lay them like shingles—butt end down in the snow at a slight angle away from you. Lay an entire row this way, then lay a row in front of them so they overlap each other, and so all butt ends are covered by the needled ends on the next layer. Lay a layer this way, then cover it with a layer of boughs. This gives you a cushioning effect, holding you off the ground a little more. The smaller the limbs, the more comfortable your nest will be.

In an emergency situation, cut boughs and lay them on the snow or ground, using the big ones, the little ones, everything stacked on top of each other until they are a foot thick. They will keep you up off the floor.

"Witches brooms" (mistletoe) works well for bedding because the needle growth is so thick. A six-inch layer will give good insulation but watch your fire by this bed.

Dead yellow pine (ponderosa pine), Douglas fir, or cottonwood provides slabs of dry bark. The bark slab makes very good insulation.

A bed of juniper or sagebrush bark not only is warm but comfortable. Strip the bark off and break it up (like you're making a tinder bundle) until it's bunched up and kind of fluffy, about six inches thick. Six inches of good dry grass or dry pine needles also works well.

Dry ground is a must to use grass, unless you have a moisture-proof ground cloth. A slab of Douglas fir, yellow (ponderosa) pine, or cottonwood bark won't soak up moisture.

Another good base when the ground is cold is an old punky (rotten) log; but it has to be dry. The tops of these logs are generally decayed, and you can level them off. It's sometimes hard to find one that's dry in the center, and if it isn't dry you don't want to use it. There's a lot of insulation in punky wood. Breaking pieces of rotton wood up and placing a layer to sleep on works to keep the cold from reaching your body.

Laying next to a dry log can add warmth because of its insulative value. Laying between a log and a small fire with insulation underneath can be fairly pleasant, even with no bag or blanket.

Fires

A lot of positive feelings are connected with a fire. Anyone lost or in a survival situation, even though he doesn't need a fire, will probably want a fire for psychological reasons. A fire is a big comfort. It provides security, and this is important. If you have a way to build a fire, build one.

Location and Preparation

First clear out an area at least five feet in diameter, possibly more; this means down to the soil, not just a layer or two of leaves and grass. In a forested area, duff usually covers the mineral soil, so clear all the duff down to the soil and away from your fire. If a spark lands in duff, it will probably take— sometimes a week or even two weeks later.

One man-caused fire in the Challis National Forest (Idaho) sat in three feet of duff and the forest fire crews had to put this fire "out" three times. The second time a high pressure pump was used to saturate the ground with water, yet the fire came out again a week later and had to be put out a final time.

If you are the cause of a wildfire, whether by accident or intention, and the U.S. Forest Service can prove it, you will be assessed all the fire suppression cost, which can be $25,000 (or more) per day.

Besides cleaning away the duff, check to make sure there are no low-hanging limbs over your fire, or any grass or brush around it. Then, put a ring of rocks around the fire to keep the fire from bouncing out. You can dig a pit, although we prefer the rocks. In a pit, it's hard for your fire to get the oxygen it needs, and you generally end up with a smoky fire. It's also hard to cook over a pit fire.

In the winter, be careful when you build a fire under tree limbs that bear snow. The snow either comes down on your struggling fire, or waits patiently until a good fire is going, then while cooking a meal, melted snow drips down your neck, in your eyes and ears, and adds the extra water you need in your stew. Either pick another area for a fire, or shake the snow off branches before you build your fire.

One cold January night (−8°F.) Larry thought he had found a great place to sleep, back under some snow-covered bushes where it was dry. He built his fire out in front, with a rock reflector behind it, stacked his wood, wrapped up in his blanket, and settled down for a long winter's night. But alas, he was roused out in the middle of the night by a great rain storm created under the bushes from the melting snow.

If building your fire on the snow or damp ground, a base of some kind is helpful. If the snow is fairly deep (three feet or more), you'll need a good base of logs. If you have a saw, prepare green base-logs (cottonwood and aspen are good) at least four inches in diameter and straight as possible, so when laid side by side, there'll be no large gaps between them. Make the base two layers, laying the top logs in between the lower logs. If you don't have a saw, lay a base of broken dry limbs. They will burn through, but will give you the base you need in snow.

Green log fire base in deep snow. Logs should be 4" in diameter. In emergency use whatever is available.

Build the base and fire on top of the snow; don't dig down to the ground. A not so fun winter camping pastime is trying to cook on, or stand around, a fire someone dug down to the ground in three feet of snow. If the smoke hanging down a-

Throw a large rock on wood to be broken. Watch rock doesn't bounce back and hit you.

Grip the wood tightly. Make sure there are no sharp points under the hands. Strike the tree or rock swift and hard. Do not use trees if possible as it damages the bark.

Burning the wood in two saves your energy.

Sizing Firewood

round the fire (due to lack of air in the pit) doesn't destroy your eyes and asphyxiate you, one of your party is bound to slide on the slippery, steep sides of the pit and into the fire—or the middle of breakfast.

A base of four-inch green logs will generally last a couple of hours—long enough to cook a meal. If you're going to keep a fire going continuously, start with base logs eight to twelve inches in diameter. Even so, the logs will eventually burn as the hot ashes fall between them, and the snow will start melting underneath. Your fire will slowly sink away, and in deep snow you'll probably need to relocate your fire.

After making a base for the fire, a piece of dead bark six inches square or larger is needed to kindle the fire. This helps the heat of the fire build up faster, and keeps small kindling from falling between the base logs.

If you're unable to find a piece of dead bark, cut a strip of green bark and set it with the outside up so you're not building a fire on the wet inside. A bundle of small twigs can be used in place of bark.

Tinder

The biggest problems in starting a fire, especially in the winter, are the cold and the wet. This is why you should carry highway flares and stick matches in a water-proof container. Carrying wood that contains a lot of pitch (pitchwood) and/or a dry tinder bundle guarantees some dry wood, and saves you the time of locating and gathering dry tinder.

If you don't have dry tinder with you, when available, dry sagebrush or juniper bark is excellent tinder. The inner bark of dead cottonwood trees is also good tinder along with dry grasses.

The dry little limbs underneath the big fir and spruce trees ignite well. They're small, about the size of pencil lead. Spruce is usually drier because it sheds moisture better and has finer limbs.

When you can't find anything dry, look for wood with a lot of pitch. Again fir or spruce trees are best. Lodgepole pine works at times, but the limbs are usually so sparse everything is very wet. Break off the dead, dry limbs right up next to the tree. If you chop into the base of those limbs, you'll usually find some pitch wood.

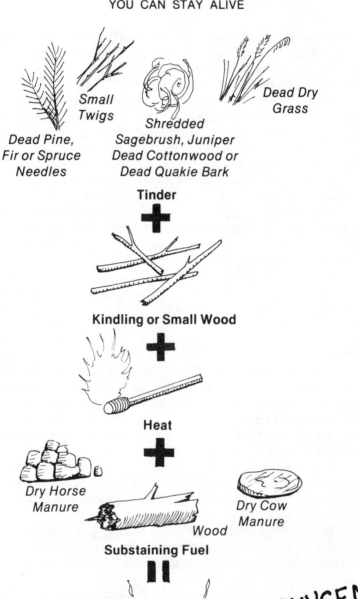

Dead Pine,
Fir or Spruce
Needles

Small
Twigs

Shredded
Sagebrush, Juniper
Dead Cottonwood or
Dead Quakie Bark

Dead Dry
Grass

Tinder

+

Kindling or Small Wood

+

Heat

+

Dry Horse
Manure

Wood

Dry Cow
Manure

Substaining Fuel

=

Fire

+ OXYGEN

Something else to look for is the small, dead, but standing trees, especially ones that have been fire killed. These contain a great deal of pitch. After gathering some pitchy wood, whittle it into shavings, pile it up, and light it. Old pitch that's hard and brittle also works as a fire starter and can be found where it seeps from a wounded tree. Soft, gooey pitch works too, but not as well. Gather several small limbs, even if they're wet. Stack them in a tepee fashion with the pitch in the middle, then light the pitch.

A good bundle of dead pine needles also works well with pine pitch. Use pine needles that have turned red, even if they're wet. Dead pine cones still hanging on trees may have pitch in them, and will work if they aren't too wet.

"Witches' broom" (a branch in an old tree that's been killed by mistletoe) is an excellent fire starter. When mistletoe strikes a tree, a big lump forms on the branch; and out of that lump grows hundreds of small branches. If the tree is still alive, you will see what looks like a large bundle of pine needles. Generally the centers of these witches' brooms are dry no matter how wet everything else is.

Rabbit brush works really well for starting a fire if you're in an area where it grows. There are two kinds of rabbit brush: a large bush up to three feet high, and a grass-like variety about eight inches high. Because of its rubber base, rabbit brush will generally burn even if it's wet or green.

On one survival trip we found ourselves standing in twelve-inch high sagebrush with rain running down our necks for the third day in a row. It was cold, and our stiff fingers were trying desperately but without luck to get some soaked sagebrush to burn. One of the students, not knowing any better, brought some of the small rabbit brush instead of sagebrush to try to burn. By this time we didn't care what anyone brought. It just felt good to hold the burning match cupped in our hands. We ignited the rabbit brush and it took! After a mad scramble for all the rabbit brush in the area, we got a good fire going. Thus, a new fire starter was born. New for us, anyway.

In extremely wet conditions, a trick proven effective in getting a fire started is to get three pieces of the driest bark you can find. Place one piece on the ground, driest side up, then put your tinder and fire starter on top of the bark. Lean the other two pieces of bark together over the top, like an A-frame, then light the tinder inside, and blow. The surrounding bark causes the heat to reflect in. After the fire starts, just blow and blow until heat builds up. Gradually poke in bigger sticks until the fire is big enough to uncover.

Reflectors

To increase the efficiency of your fire, use a reflector. A rock is the best natural reflector. We've found if you put your back next to a cliff or a rock and build a fire in front of you, the warming potential of the fire is greatly increased. Stack rocks or a wall of green logs (if you have a saw) to make a reflector behind the fire.

When you build a reflector fire, always use large rocks behind the fire and small rocks in front (between you and the fire), so hot coals and ashes won't roll down on you. Place your sleeping area one to two feet away from the close edge of your fire. If you are between the fire and a rock overhang, and the fire gets too hot, you have nowhere to go, and it's pretty hard to move a fire, especially in the middle of the night.

To maintain a sleeping fire all night, keep your wood burning next to the reflector rocks in the back of your fire. This keeps the reflector rocks hot, throwing more heat your way, and helps keep your bed of coals hotter, preventing the fire from going out so soon.

This reflector set-up enables you to warm your entire body rather than the ordinary camp fire routine of roasting the front of your body while your back chills.

Holding a Fire

A punky log works well to hold a fire overnight when you only have a few matches. Get a good, hot fire started in your punky log, then prepare a bed of dry, rotten wood, needles, or a slab of bark. This will keep the damp, cold dirt from the fire. Then turn the log so the fire is underneath the punky log. If the weather is bad, cover the log with dry dirt. A punky log can hold a spark for two or three days before bursting into a flame, so care must be taken when building a fire near one, or when using one to make sure it's completely out when you break camp. It's definitely a fire hazard.

You can hold a fire in cattle country where there are cow or horse chips (dry manure). Dry, these chips can hold a fire overnight, giving you something to start a fire with the following morning. Make a big pile of cow or horse chips (cow is best) and get a hot fire going in them, then bury them with sand or something dry to keep them smouldering during the night. You can use duff the same way.

To keep a fire going all night in the winter, gather three times as much wood as you do in the summer. Always put some wood away that's going to be protected and stay dry in case your fire goes out. Very often, even when the weather looks good, you may wake up in the morning and find a foot of snow all over.

Putting Out a Fire

When you're through with your fire, remove all the rocks, making sure they carry no sparks or hot spots; and scatter them back out again. Mix your fire with dirt. You don't need water to put out a fire. Stir it up in the dirt with a stick, making sure it's dirt and not duff or decomposed material. Stir until you're sure it's out. Scatter the ashes, again checking to be sure they're out, while working some new dirt over them, and mix it all around. If you do this, after the first rain or two, no one will know a fire was there. If you leave the ashes all piled up, it will be several years before the evidence is completely gone. And the rock ring will always be there.

Sleeping Warm

Airing

When trying to sleep warm, don't wear your clothes in your sleeping bag. This is an unwise practice for two reasons. First, with your clothes on, the body heat from the arm heats the area inside your sleeve, the body heat from the leg heats the one leg, etc. With your clothes off, the heat from your entire body fills the bag and heats everything. You end up with a lot more body heat to heat your extremities. That is why mittens are usually warmer than gloves; in gloves each finger is isolated, while in mittens you benefit from the heat generated by the entire hand.

The second reason is if you are sleeping in clothes, even just a pair of long johns, your body will give off moisture all night, and whatever you are wearing will absorb that moisture and hold it next to your body; this has a cooling effect. If you don't have anything on, that moisture goes out into your sleeping bag and away from the body.

If you don't have a good sleeping bag that can trap your body heat, you will need to wear your clothes. Before going to bed, it's very important you "air out" to get rid of moisture in your clothes. If you've been hiking and you're sweaty, take off all the clothes you can without being uncomfortably cold or running a chance of freezing. If possible, undress down to your long johns so your clothes can all air out or be dried over the fire. You want everything as dry as possible before nighttime comes and you start trying to sleep. Not only will you sleep warmer if you are sleeping in your clothes, but in the winter your clothes will not freeze solid if you take them off.

It's warmer if you take off your coat, vest, or whatever you have on, and cover yourself with it rather than wear it. Again, consolidate your body heat. The nylon or taffeta that usually covers coats and vests causes you to perspire. If you use them for cover rather than wear them, they'll fit loosely and won't trap moisture next to your body.

Hot Rocks

Whenever you're sleeping out with just your clothes and you have a problem keeping warm, hot rocks are a solution. This method is more applicable in summer, spring, or fall survival, but can be used in the winter where snow depth allows. Six flat rocks, each about a foot in diameter and about three to four inches thick, are heated by placing them close to the fire. Don't get the rocks hot, just warm. Leave three by the fire and put three under you—one for your shoulders, one for your hips, and one near your feet. As the rocks cool, rotate them with the other three. Put insulation on the ground between the rocks for more comfort.

If there is only one warm rock, make a bed of bark, grass, etc., under you and use the rock for your feet. Keep your feet warm and the rest of you will usually stay fairly warm.

Children curl up around a heated rock and sleep soundly and warm all night, but children generally sleep sounder than adults anyway.

Be careful. When the rocks are hot, they're hot! It's especially easy to burn holes in socks by using hot rocks as foot warmers. Use gloves or test your rocks for hotness before you pick them up.

When sleeping next to a reflector fire, put hot rocks on the opposite side of you so you're sleeping between the hot rocks and the fire. Rotate the rocks back to the fire so they stay warm.

One big surprise of winter is the abundance of nighttime hours, from 5:30 p.m. until 8:00 a.m. It's like going to bed after the six o'clock news instead of the ten o'clock news. When it gets dark, stay up and tell stories, lies, whatever, but don't go to bed early. Spare yourself a long 14-hour night.

Sleeping in the winter will be more pleasant if you take some cheese, nuts, or a candy bar—some kind of energy food—to bed with you. Then at 2:00 or 3:00 in the morning, when you generally start getting cold (because the temperature is dropping, and your body has burned up all its fuel to make heat), eat a little something to help keep you warm for the rest of the night. It also helps to eat something just before you go to bed.

Coal Beds

When it's cold and you only have your clothing or a blanket to sleep in, you may want to build a coal bed. Be especially careful not to build one under a rock overhang. If you build a big coal bed fire under a rock overhang and heat up the rock, chances are it can break off as it expands from the heat, or as the rock cools later in the night and contracts, it may break off and come down. Sandstone is most dangerous, but the same is true with granite or any other type of rock.

To construct a coal bed, dig a trench six feet long (or as long as your body), two feet wide and six to twelve inches deep. If possible, line the bottom of the trench with softball-sized rocks. The rocks should be as dry as possible to keep them from exploding when heated. Leave enough depth in the trench after the rocks are in place, to allow three to four inches of coals and six inches of earth over the entire trench. It can be built without rocks, but it will not hold the heat as long.

Once the trench is dug and the rocks are in place, build a fire the full length of the trench. The fire must burn long enough to build up three to four inches of hot coals. If the dirt is moist and no waterproof ground cloth is available, the dirt around the edge of the trench should be turned as the fire burns to dry it.

Tuck under legs and use a wool blanket if sleeping next to a fire.

Blanket Wrap

Dry dirt is necessary to cover the coals if a ground cloth is not available. If damp dirt is used it will cause steam to rise from the bed, which causes your clothing and body to get wet. Later, when the coal bed cools down, you will get cold.

Smooth the coals out so they are level and no high spots exist. Then cover the coals with four to six inches of the driest earth available. After the dirt is in place, cover it with a ground cloth, if possible, and then some type of dry bedding (i.e., grass, bark, etc.). Do not use too much bedding or you'll stop the heat from getting to the body.

Sleep on top of the bedding. Generally it is too hot to lay on until four to five hours have passed. If lined with rocks it will often hold heat into the next day.

If you've used a coal bed, when breaking camp, rake it open and scatter the coals and ashes, following the same procedure for a campfire. A coal bed is the same as any fire, except it has dirt over it. If a wind blows away the dirt and fans the fire, you will be responsible for leaving an open fire— without even a ring of rocks.

A coal bed should only be used in an emergency as it sterilizes the ground for a period of time.

Dig a trench 6' long, 2' wide, 1' deep. Line the bottom with 2"-3"-thick rocks.

Build a fire. Let burn 1-2 hours until 3" of coals in bottom. Level out coals.

Cover embers with 6" dry soil.

Building a Coal Bed

4
Water and Food

Water

You can live approximately three days without water. If you have water but are without food (other than what you need to maintain body temperature), you probably have at least 16 days to live.

If engaged in physical activities, you need a gallon of liquid per day, in the winter as well as summer.

Winter

Due to cold temperatures in the high country, it is usually difficult to find a source of running water. Most rivers and streams are frozen so you usually have to rely on snow. If you must eat snow or ice to get water, ice gives the most water as it is more concentrated.

If at all possible, refrain from eating unmelted ice or snow. If you are cold or haven't eaten, the intake of ice greatly increases chances of going into hypothermia. The body has to use its heat to melt the ice and snow. If it is necessary to eat ice or snow, let it melt in your mouth before swallowing. It is best to melt snow in some sort of container over a fire or in the sun.

To melt snow for use, put small amounts in your melting container. A large lump will scorch or burn, and there is nothing more foul tasting than scorched snow water! Small amounts of snow will melt almost as soon as they are in the container. As you accumulate a quantity of water, add larger amounts of snow.

A pinch of salt (no more than a pinch) will help take away the bland taste of snow water. However, you don't really need the salt. You can aerate the water by pouring it from container to container, or use it just as it is.

Stirring the snow as it melts will help aerate it and give it a better flavor.

It takes a lot of time to melt snow, especially in any large quantities, so plan for this time when you make a winter camp.

Use caution in obtaining water from creeks or rivers because of the slippery and often high edges of ice surrounding them. If you try to lean over the edge ice on a river or creek, or try to inch your way down to a creek with three feet of snow along its bank, there is likely to be one big splash—*you!* The safest way to get water from an icy or snowy bank is to tie a stick (or cord) to your cup or canteen and dip the water out. This is difficult but safe.

Summer

Preparation is the key to survival when traveling in areas where water is scarce. Carry at least one gallon of water per person whenever traveling in any dry areas.

If there isn't any water, cactus (which can be found almost anywhere there is a water shortage) contains some moisture. The best is the barrel cactus, but even the small prickly pear, if peeled and the pulp eaten, offers some moisture. You can also eat raw fruits and vegetables that contain some moisture. Sometimes it is possible to collect dew from your vehicle.

Carry water in your stomach rather than in a canteen. Anytime you're around water, drink as much as possible, then fill your containers or canteens, making sure the lids are on tight. If water is scarce, it would be tragic to waste it. The water in your body will save your life, not the water in your canteen.

People have actually died from dehydration while carrying full canteens of water. There is no advantage (other than perhaps psychological) in rationing canteen water. A sip every few hours is not going to do any good, other than wet your lips. It's far better to drink until you are saturated, then ration your sweat.

When in the desert in a bad situation, and you find a source of water, stay with it unless you have something to carry water in. If you find water, regardless of how bad it looks, it's better to drink than sit and die of dehydration.

There is a story about a man who got lost in the desert. After several days he was found lying next to a water hole, with his face an inch from the water, and he was dying. When the rescuers asked him why he didn't drink the water, he answered that he was afraid it was polluted. Then he died.

Almost any water is better than no water. If your choice is drinking "bad water" or dying of dehydration, drink the water but, if possible, purify all water by boiling at a rolling boil for 20 minutes. This destroys any contamination including the parasite Giardia. (See page 124.)

To strain insects, debris, and undesirables from the water pull a bandanna or piece of clothing tight over your mouth then put your face down in the water and suck the water through the cloth. Muddy water can also be left to settle overnight in a container.

Pothole water (old rain water stored in a hole in the sandstone) generally contains a variety of "floaters" but is usually safe to drink. In many arid, semi-desert areas most of the water you come to will contain cow manure. Just brush it aside. We've had to drink water out of cow tracks when we had no choice.

A danger sign in water is the lack of insect life. A danger sign around a watering hole is the absence of animals, or animal tracks of any kind. In this case, there is probably something wrong with the water.

Try to avoid high-alkaline water. It creates a white coating on the rocks or ground around the water. However, if that's the only water available, go ahead and drink it. Use it sparingly and don't gulp down a lot or you'll throw it up, wasting what precious liquids you had to start with. Drink a small amount, let it settle, then drink another small amount. Limit the total amount you drink.

Muddy water is all right to drink if you strain it through a bandanna, and/or let it settle overnight in a container.

If unable to find water on the surface, try digging down in a dry stream bed at the corner of bends, or under banks in low spots. If you don't come to water in a fairly short distance (two feet), you'll be better off to quit digging.

If you are not in a desert area, water is generally no real problem. In the mountainous areas there are usually springs, creeks, slough and other water sources. Again, drink whenever you can.

In the mountains, the only thing to watch for in the water is water hemlock. Hemlock creates more danger in a pond than along a stream, because the pond is stationary. There's very little danger in a running stream because the poison washes away. In fact, the only danger is broken hollow stems and roots, crushed into the water by humans or animals. The poison is a yellow oil, which may or may not be visible. In summary, boil all water if possible and drink enough to meet your needs! As stated, man can only stay alive for three to four days without liquid. It is estimated that an average adult loses two pints of water per day sitting in a room doing absolutely nothing—just through respiration and perspiration.

Food

Food is not really a necessity, but it does make for comfort, warmth, and contentment. You can, however, go off foodless, struggle through the cold, snow, and wind for several days, and probably survive. It's like going to a carnival without any money; it's a lot more fun if you take some along.

Winter

In the winter, few natural foods are available. You actually will be better off if you don't waste precious energy tramping around in the snow looking. You'll probably spend more energy looking for food you're not likely to find than the food would give you, were you to find some.

In some areas you may find tree squirrels or a few small birds, but that's about the extent of the protein. A few of the berries will stay on into winter—choke cherries, service berries, and rose hips. Tree bark is the only food available in any quantity during a winter survival experience. The inner bark of quaking aspen, cottonwood, juniper, willow, and pine trees are edible.

The Nez Perce Indians, led by Chief Joseph, lived for a month or better on tree bark as a supplement to their scanty food rations in their attempt to reach Canada, with U.S. soldiers pursuing them. The book *I Will Fight No More Forever* tells how the soldiers finally caught up with the fleeing Nez Perce and, when they went into the Indian camps, they found the quaking aspens stripped of all their bark. They couldn't figure out what had happened. Two different Indian camps were left this way. We know that for a week or two the Indians lived almost exclusively on tree bark.

To eat tree bark, first take off the thick outer bark (generally from a quarter to a half-inch thick). Inside that is an inner bark which runs from one-sixteenth to maybe three-sixteenths-inch thick. This should be leached someway to get the bitterness out. Soak it in a creek for at least one day (a problem in the winter), or boil it, changing the water two or three times. After it's leached, dry it, parch it, grind it up, add water and make cakes out of it.

You can also make a tea from the needles of the pine, fir, and spruce trees. Bring water to a boil, add evergreen needles, let it sit, and drink the tea off the needles. It isn't too bad, although it's kind of turpentiney. It will provide some nourishment and Vitamin C, which, if you were out for an extended length of time, you would need. Rose hips are also an excellent source of Vitamin C; and rose hip tea is very good.

Summer

In relatively warm weather, food is of no importance for at least three days. Almost anyone can live for two to three weeks with no food whatsoever; many have survived even longer. After three days you may need some nourishment to do much traveling; but if you think there's a chance of being found within three to six days, and you plan to stay in one area, don't worry about hunger.

If you want to spend time and energy gathering edible plants, take an edible plant class or get a good book on the subject for the area you spend your time. We list the most common in the Rocky Mountain area and how to use them.

These "incredible edibles" are very seasonal. You could be situated in a cherry orchard, but unless you happened to be there a certain two to three weeks out of the year, you would be out of luck.

When it gets down to the true aspects of surviving, and students are left to their own devices to forage for themselves for a week (with no food except "incredible edibles"), they usually choose to go hungry for the first several days. After four or five days of hunger, they spend what little energy they have left to gather edible plants. Everything gathered they throw into the common pot, and after much boiling and simmering, the proverbial "witches brew" is ready. Most of what is gathered and cooked, however, goes to waste since the students, after sampling what they have gathered, refuse to eat it.

If you're really interested in edible plants, experiment with them on a camping trip—not when you're lost and you think your life depends on them. They take getting used to.

Common Edible Plants in the Rocky Mountains

We have outlined the most common edible plants from Idaho to Arizona. Take a plant class before you're lost. Then, after learning to identify some edible plants, watch them throughout the four seasons to learn their identification in any stage of growth.

*Hardwood: Chokecherry,
Service Berry, Oak, Mt. Mahogany*

Digging Stick

Work the digging stick down beside the plant, then pry upward, working the root out of the ground.

All plant roots can be dug with a digging stick.

Bisquit Root (Lomatium): This plant is of the parsley family, which also contains some very poisonous plants such as water hemlock and poison hemlock. It should always be positively identified before it's used. The root is very bland tasting. In contrast, the poisonous members of this family are bitter and burning, or they have a strong carrot taste.

The leaves of the bisquit root smell like carrots if you crush them up. The root can be roasted, boiled, or eaten raw. Roasted or boiled, it can be mashed into cakes, dried, and then carried with you as you travel. It's commonly found from early spring until about mid-summer, depending on the elevation. The root is generally long and narrow; but it is sometimes fat like a turnip.

Dandelion (Taraxicuim officinale): The leaves can be boiled as greens or eaten raw. The older the plant, the more bitter and tough it will be. The root can be roasted, dried, and ground up to be used as "coffee." The flower buds and flower heads may also be eaten raw or boiled along with the stems. When boiling, it is best to change the water at least once on the flower heads and buds—or any other part that might be too bitter to eat—to leach the bitterness out. Then boil it again.

Oyster Plant or Salsify (Tragopogon): A first-year plant is the best, although it is harder to find because it doesn't bloom. It looks like a tuft of grass, and the roots are small but more tender. You can eat the second-year plant root also. The roots have a milky sap and are bitter. Wash them, scrape the peeling off, and boil them, changing the water once or twice.

Sego Lily (Nuttallii): The color of the sego lily flower varies. In the Superstition Mountains, in Arizona, it's a salmon-colored flower. In Utah and Idaho, it's white. Some places it's kind of a yellow, and we have heard of a blue species.

The only poisonous bulb the sego lily bulb could be confused with is *Death Camas (Zigadenus paniculatus).* Yet the growing plants are not similar. Sego lily, if you taste any of it raw, is extremely starchy, kind of gummy and sticky. Death camas is bitter, and the bulb is multi-ringed like an onion. The sego bulb has 4 rings.

The sego lily bulb can be eaten raw, roasted, or boiled. It can be roasted or boiled, mashed into cakes and dried, and carried with you. Sego lily is a hard plant to dig; the bulb is generally 4 to 6 inches deep, and the stem will break off if care is not used.

The whole sego lily plant is edible. The plant itself can be boiled. The seed pods (which are on anywhere from June to August, depending on the elevation) can be gathered and boiled. When you get into large clusters of them you can gather quite an abundance of the seed pods. Boiled, they have a flavor comparable to peas. They can be eaten raw.

Spring Beauty (Claytonia Lanceolata): This plant grows most frequently in the high country, but we have also found it in Colorado and Arizona in the lower elevations. It has a little bulb that ranges anywhere from one-fourth to one inch in diameter. It can be eaten raw, roasted, or boiled. We feel its best flavor is roasted. Again, it can be cooked, mashed into cakes and dried, so you can carry it with you. It's an easy plant to dig, generally only two to three inches under the surface. Use a digging stick. If you're in an area where there are a lot of them, you can get quite a few in a short length of time. The whole plant is also edible, either cooked or raw.

Stinging Nettle (Urtica): This plant is easy to identify if touched with bare hands, because it will cause a rash. The young plants (six to eight inches high) can be boiled as greens, and although they have a wooly texture, they are quite good. The plant can be eaten at any stage, but it grows tough and fibrous with age. Always boil before eating.

The stems from last year's plants are the best to use for fibers for making cordage.

Thistle (Cirbium Aruense): Almost all the thistles are edible, as far as we know. Peel the stem down, removing all the stickers, then cut it off near the ground. Eat it like celery. Some thistles have edible roots, too; but on some, the root is too woody and pithy to be edible.

Water Leaf (Hydophyllum): The whole plant is edible. The tops can be eaten raw or cooked as greens; and the roots can be cooked.

Wild Hyacinth (Brodiaea): This plant has an edible flat bulb, not round like sego lily, spring beauty, or onion. It has little corms around the edge. We've found it every place we've been. When eaten raw, it tastes very starchy. It can be used raw, roasted, or boiled—mashed into cakes. In some areas it is difficult to dig because the bulb is quite deep. In some sandy areas, hyacinths are easy to get, and the bulbs can be large—two inches in diameter—so it is possible to gather a lot. We found the larger ones in the fall when the plants were dead.

Wild Onion (Allium): This plant is found everywhere in one form or another. There are a lot of different species, but it's easy to identify simply by crushing the plant: it will smell like onions. It can be used raw, roasted, or boiled, and the whole plant can be eaten. If onions bother you raw, try them roasted; they are easier on your stomach.

Yellow Fritillary, Yellow Bell (Fritillaria Pudica): These bulbs are surrounded with corms, and generally aren't too far under the ground. The whole plant is edible. Its seed pods, like those of the sego lily, are edible. Some books say they should be cooked; we've eaten them raw, but not in large quantities.

Most Common Edible Plants in the Desert Areas

Cactus pads can be skinned off and the inner core eaten, either raw or cooked.

The following plants are usually found in the southwestern deserts of the United States. Generally quite plentiful in any extreme desert area, they provide food during the early part of summer and into August at the higher elevations (like in the Gila Wilderness Area).

Agave (Agave Utahensis): The center of the agave plant, the stem, when it's just a sprout (up to two feet high and six inches in diameter), can be dug out and roasted, or cooked in a steam pit. It's really quite good—kind of sweet, but fibrous. We prefer to peel it before we cook it, or it sometimes ends up with a bitter after-taste. But if it's cooked well done, it's generally quite sweet.

Yucca (Baccata): The seed pods of this yucca (which look like a cucumber or banana) are edible after you cook them. Roast them in the coals until they are well-done: otherwise they'll taste bitter. Your system has to get used to eating yucca, or you'll get diarrhea because of the soapy substance in it.

Spanish Bayonet Yucca (Yucca Glauca): Boil or roast the seed pods on the Spanish bayonet; but you have to catch them while they're young, because they dry out and pop open to drop the seeds. The baccata (above) is more like an apple; it doesn't dry out.

Barrel Cactus: The barrel cactus is used as a source of water when no other water is available. First cut the top off the cactus. You will need something long with which to cut, as the spines are two to three inches long. In a pinch, you might use a stick or rock to tear through the tough spiny outer skin into the soft pulp on the inside. The pulp has to be mashed to obtain the juice (water) from the cactus. This can be done inside the cactus plant, or chunks of the pulp can be placed in an article of clothing (a bandanna works well) and mashed, dripping the liquid into your mouth or a container.

The barrel cactus juice does not taste like water; it tastes like cactus and we don't care for it. But it will provide a good deal of moisture.

Other Emergency Foods (if nothing else is available): Any part of willows; Inner bark of quaking aspen, cottonwood, juniper, and pine trees; Pine, fir, or spruce needles, boiled into a tea, giving you a certain amount of nourishment plus Vitamin C.

Meat and large roots can be roasted directly on the coals or on a flat rock in the coals.

Cooking

Most roots and bulbs taste best roasted—on a hot, flat rock in the fire, or in the coals. It depends on their size which method is used. Put small bulbs (like spring beauty or wild onions in the Rocky Mountain area) on a hot rock. Then add some coals, mixing the coals with the bulbs.

For boiling greens like stinging nettle or dandelion, use a tin can or anything holding water. Rarely will you be unable to find a beer or pop can, but aluminum will melt if you're not careful. Fill the container with just enough water to cover the greens or stew. Set it on or in a small fire and boil.

You can also heat your container with small, hot rocks. Gather some round rocks about two inches in diameter (preferably dry rocks—not out of a creek bed) and wipe them as clean as possible to avoid extra grit in your soup. Build a log-cabin-style fire, laying layers of wood on top of each other about three high. Put small, tinder-type material between each stick of wood on each layer, to increase burning and heat. Put the rocks on top of the fire. Leave them there until the fire burns down. Try for white-hot, or at least red-hot, rocks. Pick up the hot rocks with fire tongs or a green, forked stick, and put them one at a time in the container of water. A small amount of water will boil quickly. Put only enough rocks to maintain a boil. You can cook the greens, a stew, or whatever, this way without having to set the container over a fire.

Be careful, as rocks sometimes explode as they heat. Porous lava rocks are the safest. Sandstone is no good at all.

Edible Animals

If wild edibles are too much trouble, try your hand at being a "great hunter." Except during winter hibernation, there is usually small game trapping, and some fish and reptiles can be caught. We have illustrated how to construct a basic trap and snare, and also have shown some simple methods of obtaining fish.

In the event the hunt proves successful, the easiest method is to clean (gut) the animal, leaving on the skin or feathers. Build a fire and a good bed of coals. After the coals are ready, toss the animal in. The fur, or the feathers, will burn from the animal.

Turn the animal periodically. It will take about twenty minutes to one-half hour to cook a grouse or a rabbit. When done, take it from the fire and peel off the burnt skin. Under the skin, all the juices will be trapped, and the meat will be tender and cooked.

When cooked scrape the burnt skin off while still warm.

Place the gutted bird, fish, or small animal on a small fire or hot bed of embers.

Hang the stomach or hide on a tripod with wooden skewer.

Boil in a washed stomach or fresh hide, flesh side up, using hot rocks.

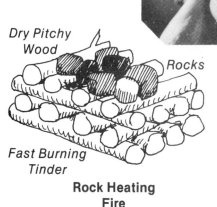

Dry Pitchy Wood

Rocks

Fast Burning Tinder

Rock Heating Fire

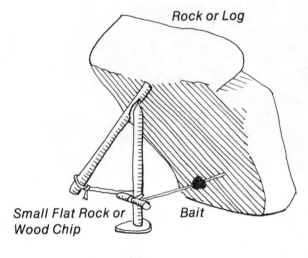

Rock or Log

Small Flat Rock or
Wood Chip

Bait

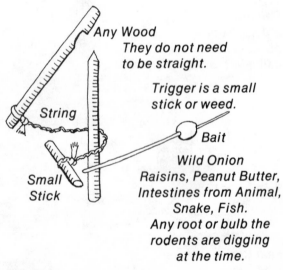

Any Wood
They do not need
to be straight.

Trigger is a small
stick or weed.

String

Bait

Small
Stick

Wild Onion
Raisins, Peanut Butter,
Intestines from Animal,
Snake, Fish.
Any root or bulb the
rodents are digging
at the time.

*Trap can be set with trigger across an animal trail with no bait.
There must be obstructions on both sides of the trail to funnel
animals into the trap. The size of trap can vary from 6 inches
high to 4 feet, depending on the size of animal.*

Piute Deadfall Trap

*Use a slip knot to
make the snare loop.*

*Rock or log weight must be heavier
than animal to be caught. It should
be hung 2 feet minimum away
from tree.*

Snares

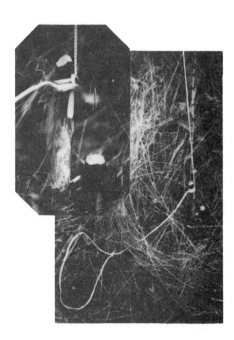

Tie with bark, string, cloth.

Scare fish downstream to trap. If alone throw rocks starting upstream. Jerk trap out when fish run in.

Willow Cone

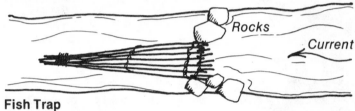

Rocks

Current

Fish Trap

Life size for 6" - 8" trout.

Set at least 6 "hooks" along the stream. Check morning and evening.

With hook parallel to line insert in bait. Point must be exposed.

Points Hardwood or Bone

Lash with green willow bark, string, cloth, sage brush bark.

Long Straight Shaft

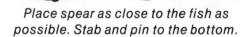

Fish Spear

Place spear as close to the fish as possible. Stab and pin to the bottom.

If over-cooked ("just right" takes practice), pulling the burnt skin off is difficult. Try scraping it off with a knife. Even over-cooked, the meat won't dry out as it does when cooked over the fire. It will be very tender and have much better flavor. Sometimes the animal won't be cooked in the middle, so eat what is done, and toss the rest back on the coals to cook.

You can stuff animals, putting the heart, liver, and other edible organs inside the animal to cook. You can stuff an animal with wild onions, sego lilies, and other edibles. After the animal is stuffed, fasten the cavity shut with a wooden pin, a stick, or whatever is available. The bulbs, roots, liver, etc., will cook inside the body.

Meat placed in the smoke will keep the flies off.

Rock

Small pieces of meat may be roasted on a stick over the coals or a small fire.

Another way to cook meat is to clean and skin the animal, and cut it into pieces as if you were going to fry it. Put the pieces on a stick. Place a forked stake on each side of the fire, forked ends up, and lay the stick, with the meat pieces, across the two forks. Keep one piece of meat, to either roast on a stick like a hot dog or toss in the coals. The pieces on the spit will be in the smoke and flies will stay away. The fire will partially smoke the meat and partially cook it. As you are ready to eat a piece, take it off the spit stick and cook it.

If cooking meat over a fire, it's best to use oak, cotton-wood, quaking aspen, willow, juniper, or sagebrush—in about that order. Sagebrush burns most quickly. Next are western tamarack, pine, fir, or spruce. All burn well, but they're so pitchy that they put a bitter, black residue on the meat. Obviously you will have to use whatever wood is at hand.

To smoke meat or fish for jerky, use quaking aspen, willow or cottonwood. Other woods either burn too fast or put a black residue on the meat, making the jerky bitter. Mix green with dry wood to maintain a smoky fire. The liver, heart, brain, and kidneys have the most food value of all animal parts. If wanting to restore your strength in a hurry, these are the parts to eat.

The liver, barely cooked, is sweet. This is the reason the Indians ate it raw as soon as they made a kill. The liver stores body glucose (sugar), and is good raw; but it should be cooked, if possible, to kill parasites. Over-cooking the liver takes away the goodness.

Eating the bone marrow of an animal provides fats and oils. A small animal such as a mouse, squirrel, frog, or small bird should be skinned, cleaned, and crushed up so the bones break into small pieces. Boil it if possible, or mash it into cakes to roast. This way you'll get all the food value from the animal, bone included.

Never eat toads; and skin all reptiles and other amphibians before cooking and eating.

We recommend if you're going to play in the woods, do as Little Red Riding Hood—take a basket full of goodies.

Jerky Drying Rack

5

Hazards

Avalanche

Thousands of avalanches, large and small, occur every winter in mountainous country, so the more time you spend snowmobiling, skiing, snowshoeing, etc., the greater your chances of being caught in an avalanche.

There are two general types of avalanches: loose snow and slab. Loose snow avalanches start small and grow in size as they descend. Slab avalanches start when a large area of snow begins to slide. The moving snow breaks away from the stable snow in a well-defined fracture line, and the snow slides all at once.

Avalanches usually occur on convex slopes of 30 to 60 degrees, but they can occur on any slope. Wind-blown snow on a leeward slope, especially when a cornice is formed, creates an extremely high avalanche danger.

Avalanche conditions are dangerous if there's been a snow, followed by a warm spell, then a cold spell. A crust forms on the snow. The cycle repeats until two or three crusts form. Then a warm sun causes the crusts under the top snow to turn into granular snow, which acts like a mass of marbles.

If you dig into snow and come to a layer of granular snow, you know you have extreme avalanche conditions. If the snow is powder or hard packed all the way down, avalanche conditions aren't as high. This doesn't mean an avalanche can't happen; but the chances just aren't as great.

Other weather factors that influence the chance of avalanche are age of the snow, wind, storms, rate of snowfall, temperature, and rain.

Age of snow: When the old snow is deep enough to cover natural anchors—brush and rocks—the new snow layers are more apt to slide.

Avalanche "chutes" with two loose snow avalanches. Only safe route on ridge top.

Slab Avalance

Wind: Sustained winds, 15 miles per hour, and higher, cause avalanche danger to increase rapidly. Winds cause snow to blow from the windward slopes to the leeward slopes, where slabs form.

Storms: Approximately 80% of all avalanches occur during or shortly after storms. Loose, dry snow slides quite easily, while moist, dense snow settles. Wind, however, can make dense snow dangerous, too.

Rate of snowfall: If snow falls at the rate of one or more inches per hour, and doesn't settle, avalanche danger is extreme.

Temperature: Snow will settle and stabilize more rapidly when the temperature is just above or at least near freezing, while a cold temperature creates an unstable condition. Especially dangerous are storms that start when temperatures are low and the snow dry; and then the temperatures rise. The first dry snow forms a poor bond, not strong enough to support the heavier, wetter snow that comes later in the storm.

Rain: As springtime approaches, rainstorms and warm winds warm the snow cover. The result is often wet-snow avalanches, especially common on south slopes or slopes under exposed rocks.

Any rapid change in weather conditions—wind, temperature, or snowfall—will cause snowpack adjustments which may affect the snow's stability and thus cause an avalanche.

In the high country, you can identify the frequent avalanche areas. These will be open strips down the mountainsides with sparse or scrubby and beat-down trees. At the bottom of an open strip you can often see piles of debris. In the winter, heavy snow covers everything, and you won't be able to see the piles of debris, but you will see a large, open area, free of timber. These areas are often at the bottom of a draw or in a big rock-slope area. Slides have stripped these areas and a person should simply avoid them.

There's a popular theory that you can skirt safely around a slide area by going up the other side of the canyon. It's simply not true!

A widely distributed movie on avalanches begins by showing an avalanche roaring down a mountain. It turns into a monster, tossing one-hundred-foot fir trees one-hundred feet in the air. A huge snow cloud rises, stirred by a fantastic wind force; the avalanche literally creates its own hurricane. The avalanche comes closer and closer to the camera, until it envelopes it.

The professional photographer (who had done several avalanche pictures) was filming from the other side of the valley. He didn't want to run the camera by remote control, and thought he was safe. When the avalanche was triggered, in a matter of seconds, it went down, across, and up the other side of the valley, burying and killing him. There really is no safe place in high-potential avalanche country, and the only precaution is to stay out.

If you must cross dangerous slopes, stay high and near the top. If you see avalanche fracture lines in the snow, avoid them. Take advantage of dense timber or ridges; they are the safest places to rest and travel.

If you have to go up or down a dangerous slope, go straight up or down—don't traverse back and forth across the slope. Avoid making loud noises; they too can trigger an avalanche.

In crossing a dangerous slope, the recommended procedure is to go one at a time, those on the sides carefully watching the person as they cross. Undo your pack and loosen your skis, snowshoes or whatever you're using so you can get them off in a hurry should you need to; and do up all your clothing as if it were super cold, so if you do get trapped in an avalanche, you can stay alive for rescuers longer without freezing to death.

Another precaution is to tie a fifty-foot colored cord to your body. If by chance you get buried, the cord will help tell your rescuers where to dig.

The new homing beepers are the best precaution in avalanche country. The unit will transmit a continuous beeping and will also home in on another unit that is beeping.

A speedy rescue is the secret to life if buried in an avalanche. The homing beepers offer the best chance of a speedy recovery.

If you're crossing the snow and an avalanche begins, discard your pack, skis, snowshoes, ski poles, etc., so you won't have anything whipping around, and begin swimming. As long as the snow's moving you can swim in it—it's fluid. The object is to tread and try and stay on top. As you tread, try to work your way gradually to the nearest edge of the avalanche, because the snow near the edge moves slower than at the center. The snow will also be pushing out, moving you out of the main force.

The moment the avalanche quits moving, it will begin to set up like concrete, and whatever position you're in is where you're going to stay. For this reason, as you swim, bring your hands up to your face and push away. Continue to do this and hopefully your hands will be moving away from your face at the time the snow sets up, giving you that much of an air space. Keep your mouth closed as you swim to avoid sucking any of the fine, powder snow into your throat and lungs.

In case an avalanche hits and the person crossing is caught in it, the people waiting should watch them as they go down, and pinpoint the last place they see them. You will need to tie that place to a reference point on the side of the avalanche (i.e., a tree or rock). The second the avalanche quits sliding, go to the reference point you set, and do a "hasty search" looking for signs on the surface. Move down hill from last seen point. If nothing is found, line up two feet apart and start probing with probe sticks (ski poles, sticks), going directly downhill from the last point you saw the victim. Time is of the essence. The only thing that's going to save the victim is your quickness in finding him. Even if he has air, he is going to freeze to death or be crushed as the snow settles! If the last point seen is high on the hill, start at the bottom working up to the last seen point.

In some cases, a person caught in an avalanche has had one arm half out of the snow, yet they were unable to move their arm in order to dig themselves out. The snow had set up!

It is estimated that a person caught in an avalanche has approximately four to six minutes to stay alive if he has no air supply, or if he has sucked snow into his mouth and lungs. This is how long you have to find a victim. In a few cases, people have stayed alive up to several hours, because they had air, and the snow didn't crush or freeze them.

Flooding

The greatest threat of flashfloods lies in the desert areas and sandstone canyon lands. Never travel in a vertical-walled canyon in sandstone country when there are rainstorms in the area. In this country there is nowhere for water to go except down the canyons. It may not be a massive flood—often only two or three feet deep—but it will be rapid and so thick with mud and debris you can hardly stand up or navigate in it. In narrow canyons, with vertical walls, the water can be far too deep for a person to survive, and there is no way out!

In Arizona, a lot of the roads don't have bridges over the washes because the water doesn't run very often. When these washes are running with muddy water, the bottom can't be seen. They usually don't appear very deep, but never drive into a wash running with muddy water unless you've checked depth first. You might drop out of sight! Several drownings a year in Arizona are due to this very thing.

Even in mountainous country, a person should check for high water signs (i.e., driftwood, debris, etc.) on the mountain sides. Be especially careful in the late spring and early summer during the high-water run-off. Depending on how far downstream you are camped, the run-off will quite often reach its peak at about one or two in the morning. The peak of heat, of course, is at two or three in the afternoon, but it takes time for the run-off to accumulate in the stream and get down to where you're camped. During the spring run-off, if you camp by a stream and you're only a couple of feet above the stream level, water can easily be in your camp before the night is over.

Check trails you plan to use along a river, especially in the springtime. See if there are signs of high water reaching the trails. Water heights are amazing. The trail may be twenty feet above the river at the time you hike in, and a week later under water. We ran a survival trip along the Salmon River in central Idaho and when we previewed the area, the river was a good fifteen feet below the trail. We came out on the same trail two weeks later wading in waist deep water. In fact, had we waited one more day, we would not have been able to come out until the river went down.

Hailstorms

There is nothing you can do to avoid such acts of nature as a hailstorm, but if you are caught in the open with no cover in a severe storm, you may receive a beating.

At one time Larry, while maintaining a trail for the forest service, was caught in a hailstorm with golfball-size stones. Fortunately he found cover under a spruce tree. At the same time his children were playing in back of the ranger station on an air strip. Before the two younger ones could get to shelter, they had large welts on their heads and legs.

Hailstones of this size could actually stone you to death if you were unable to find shelter quickly. If you see a large, black cloud coming your way, start looking for cover before it gets to you to prevent a hailstone beating.

If all preventive measures fail, and you do get caught in a hailstorm, utilize a pack, heavy shirt, coat, etc., for protection.

Sand and Dust Storms

In sand and sandstone country, a high wind can cause discomfort, pain, and injury. The eyes are the first to suffer, and grit gets in the teeth.

You can be severely injured if caught in a sandstorm without adequate clothing to protect your body. Both bare arms and legs suffer greatly from blowing sand and wind. If the storm lasts very long, it will sandblast exposed skin from your body.

On a survival trip in the canyons along the Escalante River of southwestern Utah, we were caught in high winds (40 to 50 miles per hour) that blew all day and all night. One of our party wore short pants and a fishnet shirt. He ended up with severe chafing of his legs. They were like raw flesh—extremely painful, and even bleeding.

Again, preparation is the key. Carry long pants, a long-sleeved shirt, and a bandanna to tie over your mouth. Try to find shelter from the wind and sit the storm out.

Falling Rocks

A danger in the springtime is falling rocks, especially if your trail runs along a creek or river bottom. The spring rains and runoffs loosen rocks.

When you're walking under a steep slope, the rock will fall and you'll never hear it until it lands. Other times it will hit as it comes down and you'll hear it. The natural impulse is to jump, but don't! First look and see where the rock is coming—there's as much chance of jumping into it as there is getting hit where you're standing. Look and see where the rock is, then dodge it. Don't roll rocks down the mountainside. People are killed every year because someone was having "fun."

Animals

The greatest danger from bears exists in the springtime when sows have cubs, and when the bears are coming out of hibernation (generally in April and May). They're a little more cantankerous then. Danger occurs when you get between the sow and her cubs, or when you cause a startled cub to yelp or give some other indication of danger. The sow will attack.

Watch out for cubs, and try not to pose a threat to either a sow or her cubs. When meeting a bear or some other wild animal that is potentially dangerous (such as a moose), and the animal doesn't seem excited, the best policy is to stand still and watch what it's going to do. While watching the animal, without moving your head much, look for a tree you can climb if necessary. You won't outrun any wild animal. Your hope is to reach some location where the animal can't get you.

The other danger with bears is a woman having a menstrual period is reported to have a scent similar to that of a female bear in heat. There have been several documented cases of women in this condition being attacked by bears. A recent study has confirmed this belief. The male bear doesn't really want to kill, but he's a little too aggressive in his courtship.

So far, on our survival trips in highly-populated bear areas, we have not had any problems. We ask the girls to burn their napkins or tampons, and to keep as clean as possible to keep the scent down.

The policy that seems to work best if you are attacked and there's no way to avoid it is to play dead. That's a big order! It would take strong courage to lie there and play dead while the bear mauls you. But most survivors did just that.

The black bear, in general, doesn't pose as much of a threat as the grizzly, but can be a camp menace. When camping, always hang your food in a tree at least fifty yards outside your camp, away from where you'll be sleeping. If a bear or other animal is after your food, he can get it without bothering you.

There will continue to be problems with bears until people keep and leave clean camps. Bears often feed from garbage cans and around camp grounds. As more people camp out, and bears become more accustomed to men, and to scavanging off man, bears lose their fear. There are more attacks, and more problems.

A moose is another potentially dangerous animal, especially a cow with a calf. An elk with a calf may also attack, and so might a deer with a fawn.

One thing that will get you into trouble with wild animals is a dog. A buck deer attacked a dog, who then ran back to its owner, the buck right behind it. A plain old range cow handily will take on a dog; and if the dog, like most city dogs, turns and runs back to the owner rather than out-maneuvering the animal, it brings the trouble to the owner.

Any animal, when cornered or threatened, will defend itself. To avoid trouble with any animal, don't corner it. If you do inadvertantly corner or threaten an animal, give him room to get out of the situation, if possible.

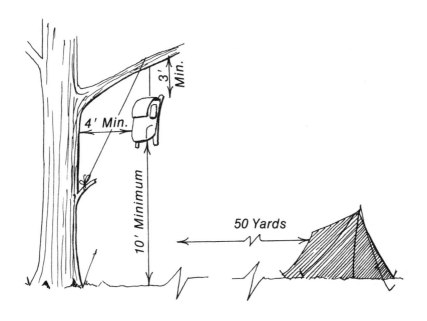

Hanging Food In Bear Country

Never leave your backpack lying on the ground or up against a tree for long periods. The back strap that cushions you from the pack frame gets quite sweaty, and rodents like to chew these up for the salt.

It is best to hang your pack in a tree. You can leave your food in it, and this also helps solve the problem of bears and other interested or hungry animals. It's quite a disaster to get up in the morning and find your provisions gone, or about six inches of your shoulder strap missing.

Ticks

Check for ticks at least once a day whenever you are in tick-infested areas, and especially in the spring. Check your scalp, armpits, and crotch thoroughly, as these areas seem to be the most preferred by your friendly tick family: Ticks, however, will attach themselves anywhere.

To remove a tick, grasp it firmly, as near the head as possible, and pull it out. If the head stays imbedded in the skin, dig it out with a needle and tweezers. Apply a liberal coat of disinfectant or antiseptic on the bite area.

A tick bite on the head (where the tick burrows into a certain nerve) sometimes causes what is called *Tick Paralysis.* The symptoms are lack of coordination; strange behavior to the point the victim seems to be mentally retarded; inability to stand up, walk, or even move the lower limbs; and difficulty in talking plainly. Sometimes the victim will become numb from the neck down.

The cure is removal of the tick. The victim should recover anywhere from a few hours to two or three days at the most.

A six-year-old boy suffered tick paralysis the summer of 1975. The tick had been on him two days. The first symptoms were fatigue and loss of appetite. On the third day, when a-wakened in the morning, he could not stand up. After falling he would laugh and roll around on the floor. His speech was slurred, and he was completely numb from the neck down. Three days after the doctor removed the tick, he recovered fully.

Another boy, ten years old, got tick paralysis the same summer. He felt sick and wanted only to lie down. His coordination was poor, and he had difficulty getting around. No one knew how long the tick had been on him, but he was better a few hours after the tick was removed from his head.

Rocky Mountain Tick Fever takes three to fourteen days after being bitten before symptoms begin. Generally a loss of appetite and rundown, flu-like feeling are the first symptoms. Then fever, headache, eyes hurt in the light, aches in the bones, joints and muscles, and confusion. A few days after the disease begins, a red rash starts on the ankles and wrists and spreads over the body. The sickness lasts a couple of weeks.

Relapsing fever begins two to fifteen days after being bitten. Fever, headache, aches and pains, nausea and vomiting and a cough are some symptoms. Sometimes a red rash will appear. This will last two to eight days, then go away for three to ten days, and unless treated, it will come back. This is an organism in the blood transmitted by the tick and can only be identified by a physician.

Colorado Tick Fever is the most common. It begins four to six days after bitten with fever, chills, headache and general aches. Eyes may hurt in the light. It lasts two days, goes away, and then comes back. As with all tick fevers, a doctor should be contacted to make sure which fever it is. Rocky Mountain fever is the most serious and must be treated by a physician.

If there is one case of the disease in an area, several more will occur during the same season. Then there will be several years with no new outbreaks. Yellow-bellied marmots (rock chucks) are one of the prime carriers of this tick.

There is a vaccination for Rocky Mountain Tick Fever—a series of three shots. It is advised for those who spend much time in tick-infested areas—which are virtually everywhere.

Insect Stings

Deaths due to anaphylactic shock caused by insect stings far outnumber deaths caused by all other venomous animals, including poisonous snakes.

Individuals have generally had minor reactions or in some way are aware they have problems with insect bites or stings. If this is the case, do not go into the wilderness without taking proper precautions.

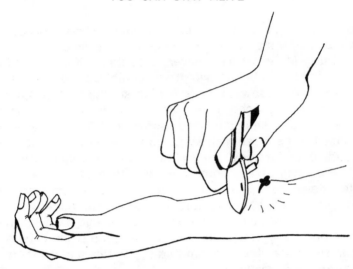

Remove a bee stinger by scraping it out with a knife blade. This method will not push any more poison into the stung area.

Symptoms of anaphylactic shock generally begin within 5 to 20 minutes after the sting. They normally begin with respiratory problems that can be severe in a few minutes. Swelling of the throat occurs and can make it impossible to breathe. Eyes may become swollen and red, nose and eyes may begin to run, and there may be a rash or reddening of the skin. Nausea and vomiting may also occur.

This is a true medical emergency and treatment must be immediate. Seconds can mean the difference between life and death.

Treatment consists of an injection of epinephrine. "Insect Sting Kits" are available on the market. Ask your doctor about them. If you are frequently in situations where you might be stung and unable to give yourself an injection (rock climbing, kayaking, etc.), an epinephrine inhaler should be carried.

Cactus Spines and Burrs

When traveling in dry areas, plants with spines and burrs can be a problem when they get stuck in your clothing. To remove them, use a comb and comb as many away from your clothing as possible. The smaller pieces will need removal with tweezers.

Snakes and Scorpions

Not threatening any animal applies to rattlesnakes, too. If you are going to be in an area where poisonous snakes are found, you should acquaint yourself with them. These include the water moccasin (cottonmouth), the copperhead, coral snakes, and rattlesnakes.

Our experience with rattlesnakes (as with most any other animal) has been that about ninety percent of the time they'll try to get away if they have a chance. But if you step on them or right next to them, or if you startle them and wake them up, they'll strike!

Give a snake plenty of warning that you're coming. Anytime you're in snake country where visibility is limited (brushy or rocky), walk heavily—stomping your feet as you walk along; or take a stick and beat the ground and bushes ahead. When going through brush so thick you cannot see snakes, roll rocks down through it or toss rocks into the brush before going through. This warns snakes and hopefully they'll give you some warning (rattlesnakes buzz—not rattle), or crawl away.

Generally, if you watch for snakes, leave them alone and don't startle them, they'll get out of your way and leave you alone, but watch carefully—they're designed for camouflage.

In the heat of the day, they're usually in the shade, because they can't stand the heat; high temperatures will kill them. They're underneath the rocks or brush, where they're hard to see.

You are most likely to encounter a snake in the early morning and evening hours, or at temperatures of 80 to 90 degrees. In Arizona and New Mexico, where the nights are warm, they're usually hunting all night. This is the time to be alert in open areas.

If possible, when in snake country, wear heavy, knee-high boots and leave your pant legs over your boots. Often a snake will strike at the pants instead of your actual leg.

If bitten by a rattlesnake (75% of all poisonous snake bites are from rattlesnakes), keep this in mind: approximately 8,000 people are bitten each year in the United States, and an average of only 11 or 12 die. Shock, from panic, kills most of the people who die. Quite often, however, the victim will end up with muscle or nerve damage in the area in which he is bitten.

The main thing is to relax. Don't panic, and don't run. Both cause the venom to enter your system quickly.

If you can get to a doctor within a half hour, apply a constricting bandage to cut off the circulation of the skin (loose enough that a finger can be inserted) between the site of the bite and the heart. As the appendage swells, gradually move the constricting bandage to areas closer to the heart.

If unable to get to a doctor quickly, go ahead and follow the cutting and suction procedure any good snake-bite kit prescribes. Don't make the incision too deep. Victims are often injured more from over-zealous cutting than from the actual bite.

Whenever you will be around scorpions, carry some of the instant cold-packs. Cold is the prescribed treatment for scorpion stings. The problem we've found with them, however, is that the packs get crushed rather easily, so pack them carefully.

The best prevention for scorpions is to not pick up any rocks or logs without first rolling them over with a stick. In snake or scorpion country, you should do this, because both snakes and scorpions like to crawl under things.

In any area where you might encounter scorpions, check your clothes and your boots before putting them on in the morning. Quite often scorpions will crawl into them.

There are three types of scorpions, one of which is considered deadly. If you get stung by the non-deadly species, the effect of the poison will be local.

The key to diagnose a deadly scorpion sting is tapping the area of the sting with your finger lightly. If it produces a prickly or tingly feeling that travels up the extremity toward the body, the deadly species is the culprit. In severe cases, the extremity becomes numb and tightness appears in the throat. The victim becomes restless and nervous. Fatal cases go into convulsions and respiratory problems.

Apply a skin tourniquet between between the sting and the heart. Apply cold pack or place stung area in a cold stream. Get medical aid as soon as possible. It is advised to carry instant cold packs or freon when traveling in the areas of the Yellow Slender Tailed species (the bottom of the Grand Canyon and southern part of Arizona).

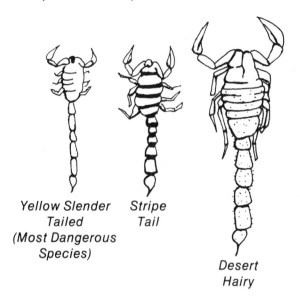

Yellow Slender
Tailed
(Most Dangerous
Species)

Stripe
Tail

Desert
Hairy

The Anti-Venom Production Lab at Arizona State University, Tempe, Arizona, makes an antidote which should be given to children and the elderly. All should be treated by a doctor as soon as possible.

Cold is the best treatment for a scorpion sting. Apply a constricting band that cuts off the circulation of the skin between the site of the sting and the heart; then apply the cold. Finely-crushed ice wrapped in a thin cloth is ideal to put on the stung area, but a cold stream is better than nothing; or the instant cold-packs are good. After the cold has been in place for five minutes, remove the constricting bandage. Immediate transportation to a doctor is advised. His care is especially urgent if the victim is a child.

6

Travel

You're stranded! If no one is going to be looking for you (you didn't tell anyone where you were going) or you feel *really* confident in the direction to go, and you can walk out in a day or two, start trucking! Otherwise, stay right where you are and wait for someone to come and find you.

It is important to find your own stride and set your own pace. Most people who do much hiking soon find their personal stride. Oftentimes when two or more people hike with each other, they try to stay right together even though one may end up going much faster than is comfortable. We have found it better to hike at our own individual pace, even if one of us has to wait for the other ever so often. Using the stride and the pace that is most comfortable for you is an excellent way to conserve energy.

As you hike along, notice areas that would make good shelters, or could be used for protection from the wind. If you get into a bad situation, backtrack to that area, knowing you will have protection there.

We have included some illustrations of methods used to make packs and carry small amounts of food and clothing with a blanket, that also can be adapted to other materials.

Orientation

Always carry a compass, winter or summer. In order for a compass to be of any value, you have to know in which direction your vehicle, destination or civilization lies. Knowing your directions won't help if you don't know which way to go.

Take a reading with the compass whenever you leave your vehicle. Get far enough away from the vehicle so the metal doesn't affect the compass, and take a reading on the direction you're going. This gives a general idea of what direction to take in order to come back and hit the road.

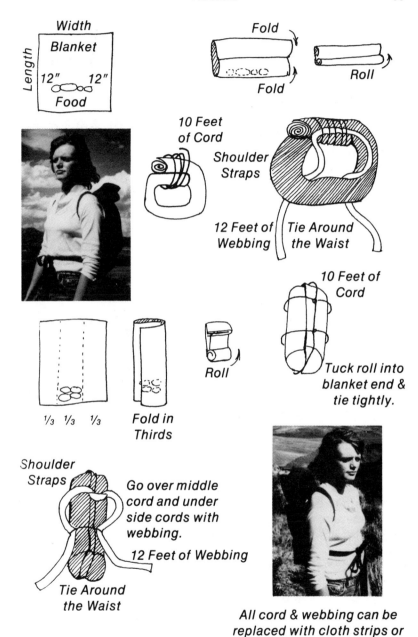

Width
Blanket
Length
12"   12"
Food

Fold
Fold
Roll

10 Feet
of Cord
Shoulder
Straps

12 Feet of | Tie Around
Webbing | the Waist

10 Feet of
Cord

Tuck roll into
blanket end &
tie tightly.

⅓ ⅓ ⅓
Fold in
Thirds

Roll

Shoulder
Straps

Go over middle
cord and under
side cords with
webbing.

12 Feet of Webbing

Tie Around
the Waist

All cord & webbing can be
replaced with cloth strips or
cordage made from natural
fibers.

Blanket Pack With Webbing

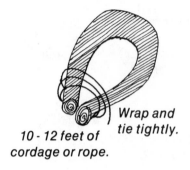

10 - 12 feet of
cordage or rope.

*Wrap and
tie tightly.*

*Roll food or clothes
up in blanket.*

*Rope, cloth,
etc., may
replace
cord and
webbing.*

*Place
bandanna
or padding
on shoulder
under cord.*

Blanket Pack With Cordage

If you know what direction to go to reach a road or civilization, but have no compass, pick some prominant point or landmark to go toward. Keep checking that point to keep your direction. Otherwise, you'll wander in a circle. People say, "I'm next of kin to Daniel Boone and can always tell my directions." Unfortunately, the record shows anyone wandering around without means of checking his directions will not go in a straight line.

Other methods of finding directions are using the North Star on a clear night or on a clear day using the stick method.

When the sun is hidden by clouds, gravel anthills in semidesert areas can give indication of directions. Ants put their openings where they get the most early sun.

In the high country, wood ants make their homes out of sticks and pine needles and don't seem to follow this pattern.

*Place straight stick vertical
in ground. Place small stick
at very end of shadow. Wait
30 minutes, place small stick
at very end of shadow.
Line drawn between small
sticks runs East-West.*

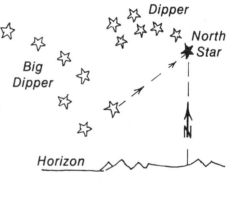

*Divide ant hill made of gravel into
fourths, placing the hill opening
in the middle of one quarter. This
will be the southeast quarter.
There can be nothing shading
the ant hill.*

Finding North

Another sign of general direction is the plant vegetation on the slopes. Plants that need more sun (wild onions, sego lilies, etc.) grow on the southern exposures. In other words, the area where they're growing gets the most sun and usually faces south, or relatively south.

If using any of these methods to determine direction, check yourself with at least six or more different tries because exceptions are common.

If you don't know which direction to travel, there is always the old standby of following the creek out. In most remote areas, however, you will have to follow that creek a long time before you come to a cabin or anything civilized.

If you do have to follow a creek out (and in some cases that's the only way to get out), stay out of the creek bottom. Climb up onto the side hill or bank, out of the brush and the jungle that grow in a creek bed. Try to stay on the south exposures of the slopes—they'll have less timber and downfall.

Snow

General Information

Traversing snow faces in the springtime is a common problem that may extend even into July in the high country. There are large snowbanks running down the mountainside 100 to 200 feet wide. The snow is usually soft, wet, and slick. These faces are generally on steep slopes. In fact, quite often they are the aftermath of an avalanche, and there's usually a big rock pile at the bottom. In slipping or sliding down these snow faces you run a risk of a broken leg or a cracked head.

Don't ever go out on a snow face unless you have an ice ax, a ski pole, or at least a stick in each hand. The sticks should be at least two feet long and one-and-a-half inches or more in diameter, sturdy and strong, and pointed on the end. Make the sticks long enough to use as canes for support while walking across the snow.

If you do fall, instead of sitting down (the normal reaction of most people) turn on your stomach and dig in with all fours, using your toes and a stick in each hand, and arching your body off the snow. If you get stopped within the first ten or fifteen feet, you've got it made. Beyond that, the momentum

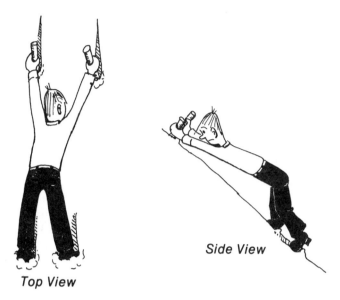

Side View

Top View

Two Stick Snow Arrest

One Stick Snow Arrest

*Either method will work on snow
that can be penetrated—not ice.*

builds up tremendously, and chances of getting stopped are
pretty slim.

It is possible to get stopped by digging in with your hands and feet, but we heartily recommend obtaining sticks before you attempt to cross any snow face.

If you do slip and manage to get stopped, to get off the snow stay on all fours. Dig in with your toes (don't go on your knees!) and your hands, sticks, or whatever you're using, and work your way carefully off the snow and back to the side.

If you run into a lot of snow, it is best to get up early in the morning, when the snow is frozen, and travel until about noon, one o'clock, or perhaps even two o'clock, before the snow starts getting soft and mushy. In the spring when the snow is really wet, you get soaked.

On the ridges, sometimes travel is continually in the snow, especially if the trail happens to be on the north side of the mountain. When the snow starts to soften up, find a place to make camp and plan to travel again the next morning.

If you hit snow faces early enough, when they're still frozen, kick steps in the snow as you go across. Again, use your sticks: cut your steps, then plant your stick. As in rock climbing, make sure a hold is solid before you put your weight on it, then move to the next one. Fall and spring snow will, at times, develope a hard crust that cannot be kicked into. The steps must be cut with your sheath knife. Be extremely careful. Without an ice ax there is no way to stop yourself if you slip.

In a situation where, walking without snowshoes or skis, you start across snow (a gully or a big drift) so deep your feet won't touch the bottom, you'll flounder. It's like walking to the deep end of a swimming pool: you go so far, then begin to float. Forward motion becomes impossible.

In this situation, get on your hands and knees so your legs, from the knees down, spread your weight out a little more, and crawl across the drift. A stick between your hands (grab a hold of each end and put it down, both hands at the same time) will give extra support and helps to spread the weight.

If the snow is really soft and none of these methods work, roll across the snow, or crawl on your belly. Plan to get very wet.

Be careful around creeks and streams. Small streams and springs will be snow-covered, and the ice on them often is not very thick. If you try to walk across the ice, you may fall through and get wet.

Be especially careful when approaching the edge of a creek or river to get water during the winter. Occasionally, deep snow may border creeks, while rivers very often have what is called "river ice" or "edge ice." On the Salmon River in central Idaho, it's not uncommon to see ice six feet thick, ending in a vertical drop-off down to the river. Under these conditions it's easy to slip or fall into the water.

If you do fall in, get out quickly and roll in the snow if it's a dry, cold powder snow. Snow itself is moisture-absorbent: rolling in it will absorb a lot of the loose water off your clothes. You must work quickly. If you're only partially wet you can rub dry snow on your wet clothes, then dust it off.

Get out of your wet clothes. Wet clothing draws heat from your body 240 times faster than dry clothing. Get out of wet boots and socks and into dry socks, dry boots, or dry something to avoid frozen feet. If possible, carry a change of dry clothing, paying particular attention to the lower half of your body, since it is usually what gets wet. Get in your sleeping bag while your clothes dry. In cold weather, get dry right away.

Snowshoes

In the winter, when up to your armpits in snow, you'd better do something to make travel easier. It's possible to wade through about three feet of snow if your legs are long enough; but any snow over six to twelve inches deep (especially with a crust) will usually wear you out, get you wet, and bring on exhaustion and possibly hypothermia.

If possible, make something that enables you to travel on top of the snow. Even if it's awkward to use, it's better than trying to drag yourself through a couple feet of snow! There are several different ways to make emergency snowshoes or skis to get you on top of the snow so you can travel with efficiency.

Snowshoes take time to make, and you generally need some kind of twine. One simple snowshoe frame, that doesn't have to be bent, consists of two sticks four to five feet long, and tied together on both ends. Put two additional sticks, each about a foot long, in the middle to hold this frame apart, and tie them securely. Take four or five sticks about as big around as your thumb and tie these close together between the two cross pieces to make a platform for your foot to stand on. With this frame you can then weave willows between those cross pieces in the frame, thus making a snowshoe without much twine. In the high country the willows are usually too small to use, so use small pine boughs.

An easier way, if you happen to have a hundred feet or so of string, is take a sapling or a small tree and bend it around, joining ends, to make a frame. You have to apply heat to the areas you plan to bend or they will snap if they are frozen. Then tie two cross pieces a foot apart in the middle, and tie a platform on them for your foot. Criss-cross your twine back and forth across the "U"-shaped frame.

Another kind of snowshoe consists of a frame—square, round, or tear-shaped—into which you weave branches so they'll hold on. These work after a fashion, the problem being the snow will get on top of the snowshoe, and you end up packing a lot of snow with each step. But they will work.

To tie snowshoe bindings and fasten your foot to the snowshoe, wrap your cord around the front stick holding the foot platform, over your toe, back down around the stick, then up across the top of your foot, and back around your ankle, then around in front of your ankle, then tie.

Skis

To make skis, cut down a dry dead tree, about three to four inches in diameter. A tree growing on the side of a hill will have a natural curve at the base you can use for the front of your ski.

Cut the trees about six feet long (or at least as long as you are tall), flatten a spot on them for your feet, and cut a groove around them on those flat areas to hold the twine. You'll need two ten-foot pieces of string or cordage to fasten your feet to the skis. Tie the skis on with a regular snowshoe-binding tie, then find a couple of other sticks to use as ski poles.

Since the skis are round on the bottom, they roll, so care must be taken to avoid twisting your ankles. The snow also builds up underneath the feet, so stop occasionally and clean them off. They might be awkward, but they save much effort in bucking the snow, and enable you to travel quicker.

Stream Crossings

The best way to cross a stream is to find a large log or some other kind of bridge. Check the log to see if it is slippery and wet, and if it's steady so it won't roll. Get down and crawl across, if necessary, rather than take the chance of slipping off, falling astraddle, or falling down and hitting your head and then tumbling into the creek.

A good way to ford a stream is to find a small tree leaning across the stream to hang on as you wade across.

Unfasten waist strap

It's Safer To Scoot Across Wet, Slick Logs.

When crossing swift currents with water knee to mid-thigh in depth and no log or tree is available, use a pole, placing it upstream from you.

The current will force your pole to the bottom. Face diagonally upstream so the current hits into the front of your legs rather than the back. A strong current from behind may buckle your knees. As you move, step into the current, placing your foot so you cross the stream either straight across the current or angling downstream. Always make sure both feet are solidly placed before you move your pole. After moving the pole, move your feet, making sure the first is planted solidly before you move the other foot.

If the current is swift and cold, and the bottom rocky, don't cross if the water depth is above mid-thigh. There's no way to keep your balance.

Use a strong stick on the upstream side. Face slightly upstream, and keep both feet or one foot and the stick anchored when moving a foot or the stick. Do not try to cross swift water over mid-thigh deep.

Crossing Swift Water

When you wade a stream, quite often your feet will ache or go numb from the cold before you get across. In a rocky streambed, the rocks will add to the pain if you take your boots off, but this is best to prevent blisters if you plan to hike after you cross the stream. A pair of socks will help protect your feet against the rocks.

When there are several people in the group, the human chain is a good method of crossing a stream, especially for smaller or weaker members of the party. Everyone joins hands by taking a hold of the wrist of the person next to him, forming a wrist-lock hold between each member, with the weaker or smaller members between the stronger or larger ones. Then, facing upstream against the current, the group slowly works its way across the stream.

If you need to get a rope across a stream, use the pole method described earlier. The rope will pull you off balance when the current hits it, and it is tricky and dangerous. Therefore, it's better to take a parachute cord across the stream, then, after you cross, pull across the large rope tied to the small cord. After the rope is across and cinched tight, tie it securely; the less experienced members of your party can hang onto it as they cross the stream.

Never secure yourself with a rope to an object on the bank, and then try to swim or wade across. If you get stretched out on the rope, you will get pulled underneath the water. The rope will bring your body back to the stream edge it is tied to, but the current will pull you down to the bottom.

7
Search and Rescue

Organizing a Search

One late summer a seventeen-year-old hunter got lost when he became separated from his dad and brothers. He was reported missing by 10:30 p.m. the same day. His dad claimed the boy had "everything" with him: a pack with food, some extra warm clothing, and matches. The brothers, who later helped in the search, said the boy knew which way was north, yet neither one of them was carrying a compass; and only one had matches—book matches. Fortunately, after three days, the boy walked out on his own in good condition. The search, however, was a fiasco!

Since the boy was reported missing at night, the search should have started at daybreak the next morning. The ranger did not arrive until 9:00 a.m., and the search didn't get started until 10:00—four valuable hours of search time were wasted.

The ranger started the search by looking for the boy with a helicopter for about two hours. This cost the dad several hundred dollars. The small B-1 helicopter used could safely haul about 400 pounds. In this case, the ranger and deputy sheriff both went up with the pilot, so the chopper was operating at the limit of its capacity. The ranger was not a trained observer; he had accumulated very little flying time. No helitack personnel (fire spotters and fighters)—no one with experience spotting things from the air—was used. The ranger did spot some smoke, but was unable to give a township, range and section description of its location. He could only give a vague description: "In such and such creek drainage," an area 12 to 15 miles long with extremely dense timber. To help the ground crews, there must be a legal description that can be found on a map.

The boy was unable to build a fire because of heavy rain. He had book matches with him which are next to worthless, especially under damp conditions. A highway flare would have started a fire in the heavy rain, and with a fire, a smoke smudge could have helped him be rescued the first day.

In the ground search, the ranger was reluctant to send anyone to the mouth of the creek on which the boy had been lost, yet that was the most logical place for the boy to show up. The father insisted the boy would not work his way down to the river because he had been told it was too dangerous. The banks of the river were too steep and rugged, and there were too many snakes. Fortunately for the boy, he didn't listen to his dad, and went downstream, then followed the river to where he found some other hunters.

Other than the fact that the boy was unable to start a fire, he did everything else right. When it rained, he huddled up under a big spruce tree, put on his extra clothes, and ate some food in order to keep up his body heat. He had a long coat, and the weather wasn't very cold, just wet.

The boy had started to make arrows out of rocks on the trail, to show which way he was going—again, a good thing to do.

Many Forest Service personnel involved in this search put in many hours and many miles—all a complete waste because of the out-of-the-way places the ranger kept sending them. One day was spent hiking around in a rain storm, only to be called back, about halfway to their destination.

Volunteer searches are often disorganized. Clearly, searches are for trained people. The person in charge may be a ranger, a sheriff's deputy, a search and rescue unit, or an experienced outdoorsman. Whoever it is, the following methods should be followed in conducting a search for a lost person.

Air Search

Use a helicopter for the initial search. Keep in mind you will have to pay anywhere from $175 to $1,000 an hour, depending on the type of helicopter used. Cover the open areas, looking for smoke or visible signs, and limit it to that to start with. The chances of spotting a body in any kind of dense timber or brush are not good.

If you, John Q. Citizen, are having a search conducted, and are paying for the helicopter, make sure the man who will be spotting (one pilot and *one* lookout, depending on the size of the helicopter) is experienced. You have the right to demand, or at least request, that someone qualified is in that ship. If an experienced person is not available, you may as well be up there flying around yourself. You will be paying for it; and have every right to be in it.

Remember, it's not just a matter of being able to spot smoke or a signal, but being able to report the exact location via radio, or pinpoint it on a map, so push hard for a trained helitack personnel member.

Ground Search

If a ground search is being organized in the mountains, request searchers to start the initial search by placing a person on each ridge of the drainage so they can follow the ridges down to wherever the drainage hits the main river. As they work their way down, they should look for signs or tracks. If there are enough people, have somebody work the bottoms too; but bottoms are hard to cover because visibility is limited and growth is thick. People on top of the ridges going down will have more visibility; and the ridges are quicker and easier to cover. Generally, some of the people on the ridges will end up on the bottom anyway, because the ridges will drop down into the bottoms and fade out. If the terrain of the ridges are too rugged for travel, another system must be used.

There have been instances where a lost person went cross country, but most people eventually end up coming down a drainage. Place someone at the mouth of the drainage in case the victim comes out.

Be wary when someone keeps guessing: "I think he'll do this." There may be some value in asking, "Where would I go if I were him?" but realize in doing this certain assumptions are made; the lost person is *not* injured, he *is* rational, etc. These assumptions imply a risk. The victim may be injured, lying somewhere shot, or with a broken leg—whatever. It's hard to outguess someone when his circumstances are unknown. You don't know if his thinking is rational.

Manpower at the beginning of a search is vital. The first two or three days are the critical days in a search operation. Often, expecting the victim to walk out, organizers don't get excited on a search until the second or third day; then they start calling in the manpower.

If you are concerned enough to call a search (knowing you will be paying all or part of the searchers' wages while they are out looking, paying for a helicopter, etc.), you must be worried.

You have full right to expect some manpower. Push to have a real search conducted. Get a lot of men at the beginning.

If a lost person is going to panic or go into hypothermia, it will be in the first few days. If he knows enough to keep himself alive the first few days, he should be able to stay alive at least a week or better.

If they are not found by the helicopter or quick ground search, a systematic search of an area should be done on a grid system. To cover an area in a systematic grid, searchers have to line up within visibility of each other; if that means ten feet apart, that's what has to be done. Unfortunately, you're not only looking for a person, you're looking for a body, and if you can't see beyond ten feet, then searchers need to be that close together. An area hasn't been covered unless it's been covered with a grid system.

Hopefully, a properly-conducted search will save lives and dollars. Searches often mount up to thousands of dollars. That's bad enough, but a hundred times worse when the whole thing is to no avail.

Aiding Rescuers

When deciding whether to stay put or try to walk out, if lost, *stay put.* If you knew which way to go, you wouldn't be lost. In the summertime you can have a great time thrashing around the woods, telling yourself you really know where you're going, and your compass is broken or gone wacko; but in the winter this kind of behavior could end in your death.

The only movements a person ought to make are those to signal searchers or those necessary to adapt for survival (locate or make shelter, find firewood and water). These are the things you'll need to do to stay alive. Most people who survive to be found stayed put and let rescuers find them.

Signal Fires

When possible, move to a high ridge or clearing and build a large fire—a smoke smudge—to attract the attention of possible rescuers. Cold air in a canyon won't rise; smoke settles, so you should be on a ridge before trying to signal. Letters spelled out are also more likely to be seen up on a ridge. In the summer, any billowing smoke will probably be spotted by a lookout, but in the winter there are no lookouts to see the smoke, only a possible airplane. Start the smudge as soon as you hear a plane so hopefully the smoke will be as big and high as possible when the plane gets to your area. The standard distress signal is three columns of smoke; but if you're all by yourself, three good columns of smoke may be more than you can manage. At night, if you hear airplane activity, you could get and keep three smaller fires going. A fire at night will show up a long way, especially if it's up on top of a highly visible ridge. We've seen ordinary-size fires as far as fifteen miles away at night.

In the daytime, it takes a lot of smoke to be spotted from the air. On our survival trips we usually have air drops to bring in supplies. Often our people on the ground think they have a really good smudge going, but those in the air can barely see it; and they knew our exact location in advance.

In winter the regular smudge from burning green vegetation might not show up against snow, especially on a hazy day, so try to throw up as much heavy, black smoke as possible. If you're by a vehicle, burn one of your tires or part of the seat to produce a black smudge.

You can use pine boughs or some type of green vegetation if nothing else is available. Pine boughs don't put out much black smoke, but they do put out a darker, heavier smoke. Pitchwood (wood filled with pitch) puts out a very dark smoke.

Rabbit brush, with its rubber base, also puts out a more visible smoke. Green rabbit brush makes the darkest smoke. In the summer a white smoke from evergreen boughs will contrast with trees or green meadows.

In the winter, smoke won't go up in a column; the cold air holds it down. So unless it's black smoke that will show up against the snow, there isn't much chance it will be seen from the air. This is another reason you should start your fire on a ridge if possible. In early morning or late evening in the summer, smoke does not rise and must contrast with surroundings.

We know of many cases where people (especially hunters) won't start a smudge fire because they don't want anyone to know they got lost. It's a point of pride. However, pride should be a small consideration when thinking of the heartache, grief and worry, as well as the money you may be costing your loved ones. It would be nice if a certain amount of status were involved in quick rescue because the lost person was smart enough to know how to aid the searchers, saving money, time and worry.

Ground Signals

When marking out signals on a sunny day, tramping the S-O-S or H-E-L-P in the snow will show up as shadows to someone flying over. On an overcast day footprints will never show up, so use pine boughs or something that contrasts with the snow. In the summer use rocks or pine boughs if they contrast with the ground cover. Make the letters big (about 20 to 30 feet tall and 10 feet wide), or they won't be seen from the air. In the air, a full-sized blanket, whatever color, looks the size of a postage stamp. Doing air drops at 500 feet elevation, we've spotted red blankets and gear laid out, but they just looked like specks below us. The only reason we saw them was because we knew exactly where to look ahead of time.

Getting spotted from the air is a difficult task. On the ground looking up the plane seems so close, but visibility from a plane is never very good, and it is impossible to look straight down. Planes also go too fast.

Wear clothes of contrasting colors. Don't wear a green shirt; it would be better to remove your outer shirt, unless it's bright, and wear your undershirt.

Don't become too discouraged if a plane goes over and doesn't spot you. Most pilots don't spend much time searching the ground, so there's always a greater chance of being missed than of being seen. Don't panic, and don't give up. There will be other planes and other chances for rescue.

This again goes back to preparation. You should always tell someone where you are going and when you expect to return. If no one knows where you are, and you are sure no one will be looking for you, you may have to get out on your own.

8

Preparation and Prevention

Planning and preparation are the two keys to survival. *Rule Number One: Tell somebody where you're going and approximately when you expect to return.* Then, if you get hurt, lost or in a bad situation, someone will be looking for you, and they will know where to look.

Rule Number Two: Any time you go out (especially in the winter) be prepared to spend at least one night. When you turn off the ignition key, there is a chance your vehicle won't start again. If you are winter camping, or even hunting, and a stretch of cold weather hits, you may come back and find your battery dead. It's best if you park on a hill, facing downward, so you can give your vehicle a push and get it started (provided it has a standard transmission).

A bad experience is to be 20 miles into the wilderness in three feet of soft snow, wake up in the morning, notice you received another foot of snow during the night, and have the nightmarish realization that you laid your snowshoes, your pack, and all your life-sustaining gear "somewhere" the night before. Then you spend the next few hours wallowing around in four feet of snow, digging up every little hump and every little rise, trying to find the equipment.

In the winter, never lay anything down. If you're doing any traveling in deep snow, snowshoes or skis are a necessity. Skis should be stood on end (stick them in the snow) and snowshoes hung in a tree. There's always a chance a porcupine or other animal will chew the rawhide out of the shoes if they are standing up in the snow. You should hang everything else out too. Store all your gear in your pack and hang it in a tree. Remember, in the winter especially, your life depends on the equipment you have with you.

Anytime you venture out in the cold, you should have sufficient winter equipment to spend at least one night. Hunters are some of the worst offenders of this rule. They drive along, spot a deer on a hillside, jump out, blast away, hit one, charge up the mountain, end up traveling several miles, get lost or exhausted, spend the night in nothing, and are never heard from again, except in an obituary.

Part of your preparation for an emergency is planning, and knowing what kind of clothing and equipment is necessary.

Equipment

The following list of gear is adequate for any outdoor activities. With the exception of a few articles which are strictly for winter (designated by an asterisk), we recommend you carry most of these items with you every time you venture into the outdoors.

A sharp knife and a sharpening stone. The knife is a basic necessity. A dull knife is more dangerous than a sharp knife. A sharp knife is an efficient tool while a dull knife is dead weight. Learn the proper way to keep a knife sharp, and always carry a whetstone with you as basic gear.

Stick matches in a waterproof container. Some of the new butane lighters are very popular. They float in water, but will not light until they are completely dry, generally after several hours. They also will not light if the temperature is below 32 degrees. We personally prefer matches in a good, waterproof container.

Some kind of a fire starter—highway flare, an oil-gas mixture, a candle, or a commercial fire-starter product.

1. Highway flares are easy to carry. A ten-minute flare will burn long enough to start a fire with about anything. No matter how hard the wind is blowing, the flares will start a fire. They also work as a signal.
2. Gasoline is highly volatile and dangerous and burns so quickly that it really doesn't start a fire, At times, oil is hard to get started, especially if it's cold. a 50-50 mixture

of gas and oil is generally a pretty good combination. In an emergency, you can find both of these in your automobile.

3. A candle will work if there isn't a wind. Make a shotgun shell candle or a tunafish can candle (sometimes called a "buddy burner"). The buddy burner can be used for heat to cook over or to melt snow in a snow shelter, and is reuseable.

4. Military fuel compressed trioxane is excellent to start a fire under wet or windy conditions.

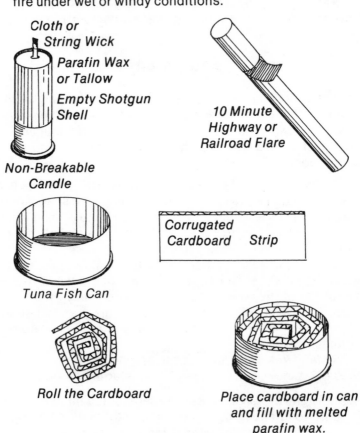

Cloth or String Wick
Parafin Wax or Tallow
Empty Shotgun Shell
Non-Breakable Candle

10 Minute Highway or Railroad Flare

Tuna Fish Can

Corrugated Cardboard Strip

Roll the Cardboard

Place cardboard in can and fill with melted parafin wax.

Place the cardboard ¼" above
can & wax to light as wick.

Fire Starters

A compass is a must. Don't buy one and stick it away in your pack; learn to use it. Whenever you leave your vehicle, take a compass reading. It may save your life.

Nylon parachute cord, a couple of pieces, each about ten feet long, is a necessity, especially in the winter (to make snowshoes). For the real survivalist, nature has provided a number of things with which to make cordage, but for most of us, it is probably wiser to bring some cordage along. It can be used for at least one hundred things, including shelter construction.

A groundcloth, preferably waterproof nylon or canvas. If you're not going to be sleeping in a tent, a plastic groundcloth becomes a problem in winter camping. If it gets cold, it gets brittle and, if you're sleeping on a snowy slope, you might wake to find yourself tobogganing to the bottom of the hill. A rain poncho can double as a groundcloth. A space brand "Emergency Blanket" (a thin, plastic sheet coated with silverized reflector) is inexpensive, compact (small enough to fit in your pocket), and waterproof; and can be used as an emergency signal and an emergency groundcloth.

A canteen or, in the winter, something to melt snow in. A canteen works well in temperatures above freezing, but in conditions below freezing, canteens freeze up, generally in the neck, so the water won't come out. Wrapping the canteen in newspapers or foam pad will retard the freezing process. The World War II G.I. canteen cups are good to melt snow in and easy to carry.

Food. In a survival situation, food is about last on your list of priorities; however, that doesn't mean you should starve needlessly. In the winter you burn more energy to maintain your body temperature. A person should have granola, candy, or a nut mix for munching to keep some energy coming in while they buck the snow and fight the cold. A canteen with a protein powder juice mix gives you liquid along with the natural sugar and protein. The best types of food in the winter are fats and oils. They burn the slowest, last the longest, and give you the most body heat per ounce. On mountain and arctic expeditions, men often take bacon bars and cubes of margarine, and eat them all day long to give them the energy they need. Next to fats and oils, protein is the best source of energy. Something with sugar gives a quick burst of energy; but burns the quickest. A sugar and protein combination offers a quick burst of energy plus a longer lasting effect. An example of an excellent winter trail food is peanut butter, honey, and powdered milk (dry) mixed together and frozen into balls.

*A wool blanket or sleeping bag. For dry conditions there is nothing warmer than a good down bag. If you are going to be getting wet, a PolarGuard, Dacron II Hollofill or thinsulate bag retains almost all its warmth, even under wet conditions. A good wool blanket is also fairly good when wet.

*A foam pad adds greatly to warmth. There are several types. The most common is a loose cell (open-cell). It's comfortable, but near water it becomes a sponge, and is hard to dry out. It also needs to be dried in the morning because your body moisture goes into the pad.

Another is a solid (closed-cell) pad. It is generally only one-quarter to about a half-inch thick and absorbs no water at all, so it's great for anytime you're going to be in damp or wet conditions, especially in the winter. A closed cell foam pad works extremely well in the winter to carry for emergencies. It insulates from the cold ground or snow and keeps you dry.

The most comfortable sleeping pad is the combination open cell foam/air matress. The foam pad is inside the air matress material. It is soft and warm. The only drawback is weight and cost.

*Tent—If doing extensive camping (especially in the winter), some kind of tent is necessary; but realize in the winter a tent is a cold shelter. A snow shelter of some kind is much warmer. However, you can get into snow conditions where you really can't use the snow to build shelters. Rain or warm weather destroy snow shelters. There are areas where there isn't material to build a shelter, and you still need some kind of protection.

A nylon, waterproof poncho can also be used for a shelter, but a little backpack tent is a good investment for any camping, especially winter.

Several produce bags to pack out trash. There's no weight involved, and the trash won't take up as much room in your pack as it did originally, so you definitely have room for it. Plastics and aluminum containers won't burn completely, and any campsite should always be left as you found it. Produce bags also come in handy for other things, and are light and easy to carry.

Backpack stoves—Stoves aren't a necessity, but a good one is quicker and easier than an open fire, especially in the winter. In heavily traveled areas, you don't have to worry about finding firewood and further depleting nature's resources. If your gas stove burns with a yellow flame instead of blue, it isn't getting enough oxygen and is giving off carbon monoxide which could poison you.

First aid kit—a necessity anytime. A first aid kit is a personal thing; you should carry what experience has shown you need. The following are some recommendations:

● Three two-inch compress bandages.
● One triangular bandage (or a four-inch compress) to hold up a broken arm or cover a large cut.
● Six band-aids at least three-quarter-inch wide.
● One pair of tweezers.
● Steri-strips.
● Ten to fifteen feet of 90-pound test fish line.
● A small, razor-sharp pocket knife. Some people carry scissors and/or a razor blade; we prefer a pocket knife because it's easier and safer to carry. Fold up scissors are good.
● Three needles and a couple safety pins.
● A one-inch roll of adhesive tape. This can be wrapped around the pill bottle or whatever you use to carry the pins and needles.
● Two-inch wide gauze roll.
● Antiseptic soap.
● Thread—pure silk button thread (works well for butterfly stitching).
● Jar or tube of anti-bacterial ointment.
● Bottle of necessary pills: aspirin, salt pills, penicillin or tetracycline, diarrhea pills (Lomotil are very small and easy to carry), darvon, ascodene, and any anti-allergy pills you may need.
● Snake bite kit, except in the winter.
● A copy of *Primitive Medical Aid in the Wilderness,* a small pocket book put out by Life Support Technology.
● *Medicine For Mountaineering,* a complete guide to mountain medicine.

A candle lantern—It can be used outdoors in the wind; or it can be lit in a snow cave to warm the shelter, and also give light. A flashlight operates on batteries, and the number-one enemy to batteries is cold; so a flashlight is useless in the winter. Besides, it's heavy to carry. A candle lantern is much more efficient.

A couple of large rubber bands are handy to use as pant guards for keeping snow out of your boots. (Garters or anklets will do the same thing.)

A saw—For winter camping you should have a saw to cut base logs for the bottom of your fire. There are small saws on the market that will fit in a scabbard on your belt.

Toilet paper is kind of a necessity in the winter. In summertime, it's just a convenience; but in the winter a snowball gets a bit tricky, and snow is about all you can find.

Clothing

Because preparation is so important (especially in the winter), the following is a list of the clothing we feel is necessary for both survival and comfort. Choose the clothing best suited for the season and terrain.

● Long johns—thermal shirt and thermal pants (wool for winter), sweat pants, or warm-up pants. It's a good idea to pack an extra pair of thermal pants in case you get wet.

● Long-sleeved wool shirt, and T-shirt for summer.

● Long-legged pants (wool for winter). Inexpensive wool pants are available at thrift stores or Army surplus stores. Select wool pants a size or two larger than you normally wear, not only because of the clothes you will wear underneath, but for more freedom of movement. If your pants have cuffs, remove them. They collect snow. Take an extra pair of wool pants in the winter in case you get wet.

● Boots—a comfortable hiking boot with a vibram sole in the summer. The only waterproof boot for winter is a rubber boot, because a leather boot, no matter what it is treated with, will eventually get your feet wet.

● A warm, wool stocking cap (a face mask).

● Dark glasses—sun glasses or tinted goggles.

● A warm jacket—we prefer a hip-length coat; one that is light to pack and that offers good insulation per pound. An extra lightweight jacket or a down vest is also handy.

● A waterproof poncho or parka to help keep you dry. A large plastic garbage can liner can also be worn to keep out rain.

● A wool scarf or a large bandanna for your neck.

Gloves or mittens for working around a fire, building shelters or just keeping warm. Mittens are best in winter to wear while traveling and for general use. An extra pair of wool gloves are useful if use of your fingers are needed. When working in the snow or with wet material, wool is a necessity.

All bodies sweat, even when inactive or in the cold, which is why both wool and down clothes are good protection against the cold. Down breathes and allows perspiration to move away from your body so it doesn't cool you. However, if you get wet, soaking wet, down becomes worthless as it loses its loft and mats up. Wool, on the other hand, retains approximately forty percent of its insulative value when it is wet. Other excellent materials are the synthetic fibers known as PolarGuard, Dacron II, Hollifil and Thinsulite, which maintain almost all their warmth when wet.

Darker colors are warmer if there's any sun to be absorbed. Of course, if you're observing game, you are less visible in a light or whitish-green color.

Winter clothing should be loose fitting so there are air pockets. It is the pockets of air between the layers of clothing that insulate from the cold.

One of the common mistakes of winter camping is clothes freezing. One particular thing to watch for is snow boots with felt liners. When people take them off at night, the felt liners, wet from the moisture of the feet, freeze; or even worse, hikers fail to remove the felt liners from the boots, and the liners freeze inside the boots. They freeze so stiff the foot will not go back in the boot. Once they're frozen in the boots, they won't come out, and it is almost impossible to thaw them out. Generally this type of boot (the snowmobile boot especially) has a nylon upper part which will melt if you get it too close to a fire. Even with the liners removed, it takes a long time to thaw the liners enough to get the foot in them. The felt liners either have to dry before you go to sleep, or put them in bed with you so they don't freeze.

Another common problem is the snowpacks with zippers. Leave the zipper up—slip the foot in and out; because if unzipped, and it freezes, you will be unable to zip it up again.

Some snowpacks (or rubber boots) don't have a felt liner; but the boot will still freeze, although not so solid you can't put your foot in it. Once the frozen boots are on, wear them awhile, and soon they'll thaw out to where they're flexible.

Be careful not to let the clothes freeze. Many people wear cotton pants and levis, which after a day in the snow get soaking wet. Hikers take them off, hang them up by the fire, and then go to bed. Of course the fire goes out and in the morning these pants are frozen solid! Climbing out of a warm sleeping bag and trying to get into a pair of stiff, frozen pants is a shocking experience. Wool clothes are a little easier to get on—they don't seem to set up as hard as the cotton—but they're still a thrill!

A group Larry took out on a winter campout wore snowmobile coveralls. In the morning the coveralls with knit cuffs on the sleeves could not be put on because the knit cuffs were frozen solid and their hands would not go through them.

If clothes are still damp when going to bed (not sopping wet), it's best if they are put underneath the sleeping bag to keep them from freezing.

Can Your Children Survive?

The reason we touch on children's survival is an experience Larry had that really made him stop and think. He was out in the wilderness, twenty miles from anywhere, alone with his five young children. He had four-wheeled into the remote area, and none of his children were old enough to drive. While enjoying a very pleasant camping experience with them, he became extremely ill, to the point he thought he might die. After he recovered, he began asking himself, "What if . . .?" Could his children have gotten out on their own, or would they have died of exposure or hunger?

A survival instructor experienced a bad accident while out with a group of about twenty students. He fell and broke bones in both his legs and feet. The accident happened in the evening, and the three students he selected to hike out to bring rescue were unable to leave until the next morning. They hiked a full day to reach help. Their instructions were to contact a certain doctor who was familiar with the area, and who would know exactly where the accident had occurred. The doctor, unable to leave until the following morning, took a full day to hike back in. The instructor was in severe pain for a full forty-eight hours before medical assistance finally came.

The question is this: If no one had been available who knew the area, could the students who hiked out have directed the rescuers to the correct location of their instructor?

As an experienced hunter, backpacker, cross-country skier, whatever, you enjoy certain outdoor sports, and hopefully enjoy these sports with spouse and children. It's not pleasant to think about being in a circumstance where you couldn't help your children, but the possibility exists. If something happened to you in the wilderness, would your loved ones be able to find their way out? Would they be able to survive? Would they be able to find rescue for you, and, as importantly, direct the rescue back to you? Are your children acquainted with maps, compasses, or the terrain of the area? Are they able, without panicking, to deal with an emergency situation that might come up? Do they know what to do?

If you feel your oldest child is old enough and responsible enough to handle an emergency, share *all* your outdoor knowledge with him or her.

Children are capable of doing much more around a camp than we usually give them the opportunity to do. Most five or six-year-olds can gather rocks to make a fire ring, gather wood and tinder for making a fire; and, under proper supervision, build and start their own fire. Children shouldn't have matches to play with, but they should be taught to use them safely when they are old enough.

Children should also be taught to build some basic shelters, learning the importance of getting out of the wind and wet. They should have some instruction on the differences between a fire for cooking or warmth, and for signal. Then they could find shelter and get a smoke smudge going, and learn to "sit it out" in case of an emergency.

Again, it's important to leave information on your whereabouts and time frame with a friend. If your children are not yet ready for this responsibility, any wilderness adventures should involve at least two responsible adults—someone you could count on under any circumstances.

As sad and tragic as it is for an adult to die in the wilderness, the sadness would be compounded if his or her innocent children were to die also, because they were suddenly left alone, without proper training and teaching.

* * *

As stated in the preface, this book was written from a positive viewpoint. It is our hope it will allow more people to enjoy and feel the peace and beauty of what our culture calls wilderness.

We hope, by giving people information to keep them alive in an emergency, they will feel more at ease in the wilderness and will spend more time in it.

Hopefully more people may come to know the wilderness as Chief Luther Standing Bear, of the Oglala band of Sioux, states in *Touch the Earth:*

> We did not think of the great open plains, the beautiful rolling hills and winding streams with tangled growth as "wild." Only to the white man was nature a "wilderness," and only to him was the land "infested" with "wild" animals and "savage" people. To us, it was tame. Earth was bountiful and we were surrounded with the blessings of the Great Mystery.

Chief Luther Standing Bear further stated:

> The old Lakota (Sioux) was wise. He knew that man's heart away from nature becomes hard; he knew lack of respect for growing, living things soon led to lack of respect for humans too. So he kept his youth close to its softening influence.

We hope *You Can Stay Alive* will allow more families and more people to safely spend time close to the softening influence of the wilderness, gaining the peace and understanding available there.

1. Break fibers out of dead stalk.

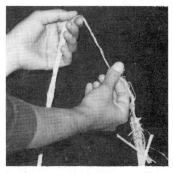

2. Clean out debris and roll fibers.

3. Two strands between thumb and forefinger strand behind pointing up.

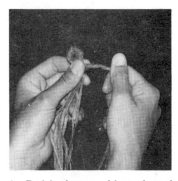

4. Behind strand is twisted away from your body.

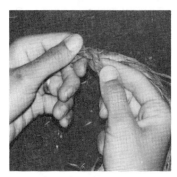

5. Then laid over the front strand towards you. Bark must be damp.

6. To splice in new strand, over lap and continue twisting.

Giardia lamblia is an intestinal protozon. It has become very common in wilderness streams and water sources. Because Giardia has a two-stage life cycle (one of which is in a hard shell), it can live in cold running streams for about two months.

In the cyst stage the germ, in the hard shell, is released in human or animal waste and carried into the water source. When the water is consumed by human or animal, the cyst attaches to the wall of the small intestine, usually in the duodenum, and the body heat causes the Giardia to enter its reproductive troph cycle. This brings about the sickness and more cysts.

Symptoms: Symptoms usually appear after 12 to 15 days. The most common symptoms are cramps and diarrhea. The diarrhea often alternates with constipation. Gas, bloating and offensive smelling stools are common. Nausea, low fever, vomiting, foul-smelling belches and headaches may also occur. In severe cases the victim becomes very ill and experiences a loss of appetite and weight.

Treatment: A stool sample must be examined by a laboratory for positive identification of the Giardia cyst. Quinacrine (mepacrine) hydrochloride taken orally (0.1 g—three times daily) after meals for five to seven days results in an 80% to 95% cure rate. More treatment is often necessary.

Chemical water purifiers will not kill this parasite. You must boil the water or use one of the filters specifically designed for Giardia.

Some people do not show symptoms but are carriers of the parasite.

Index